100 GREATS

SWANSEA CITY
Football Club

100 GREATS

SWANSEA CITY
Football Club

COMPILED BY
PHIL SUMBLER & KEITH HAYNES

The History Press

First published in 2005
Reprinted in 2011

The History Press
The Mill, Brimscombe Port,
Stroud, Gloucestershire, GL5 2QG
www.thehistorypress.co.uk

© Phil Sumbler & Keith Haynes, 2005, 2011

The right of Phil Sumbler & Keith Haynes to be identified
as the Authors of this work has been asserted in accordance
with the Copyrights, Designs and Patents Act 1988.

All rights reserved. No part of this book may be reprinted
or reproduced or utilised in any form or by any electronic,
mechanical or other means, now known or hereafter invented,
including photocopying and recording, or in any information
storage or retrieval system, without the permission in writing
from the Publishers.

British Library Cataloguing in Publication Data.
A catalogue record for this book is available from the British Library.

ISBN 978 0 7524 2715 7

Typesetting and origination by The History Press
Printed in Great Britain.

About The Authors

Keith Haynes

Keith Haynes started writing on the subject of football in 1998 after many years pottering along in the fanzine scene. In 1998 he compiled his first book, controversially titled *Come On Cymru*. For the first time Welsh football was to be represented with fans' points of view away from the capital city of Cardiff, and many didn't like it. The success of this book meant a follow-up and this came in the form of *Come On Cymru 2000!* He has also previously written on a regular basis for *FourFourTwo* magazine as well as the now-defunct *Total Football* magazine. Keith lives and works in Gloucestershire with his family and can still often be seen on the terraces watching the Swans, who he has followed as long as he can remember.

Phil Sumbler

Phil has followed Swansea for most of his life and has attended countless numbers of games. Despite living away from Swansea for nine years, he still travelled back on a regular basis with members of the MAGS to attend games and the highest point surely has to be that magical day in 1994 when the Swans played at Wembley for the first time. At present he lives in Margam with his family, who he is slowly inducting into life with the Swans. In his spare time he runs the www.jackarmy.net website – one of the most popular lower division sites on the internet, together with editing the Swansea City fanzine *A Touch Far Vetched*.

Keith and Phil have previously worked together with Tempus Publishing on *Vetch Field Voices* and their second offering *Another Day at the Office* – a biographical account of Wales' international goalkeeper, Roger Freestone. They are also currently working on *The Tony Ford Story* – a biography of the outfield player with the most all-time league appearances. Both Keith and Phil are football fans who have thrust themselves to the forefront of Welsh football writing, much to the disgust of the established fraternity who consider themselves to be the final word on relevant football matters. They continue to seek out worthy subject matters to write about.

You can contact Keith by writing to him at RY Media, PO Box 19, Gloucester, GL3 4YA. Or you can e-mail him at the-voice@the-mags.fsnet.co.uk

You can contact Phil by e-mailing him at phil@sumbler.freeserve.co.uk or write to PO Box 109, Port Talbot, SA13 2XA.

Keith and Phil would like to thank the following people, without whom they would have struggled to complete this book:

Colin Jones, Stuart McDonald, Swansea City Football Club, the *South Wales Evening Post*, *Western Mail & Echo*, our friends at BBC Wales, Lorraine Corbett, Clive Hughes, our families for putting up with us while we pieced it together, readers of www.jackarmy.net and www.scfc.co.uk, James Howarth at Tempus Publishing, Mark Griffiths at the Wrexham fans' website and finally the 100 people that gave us something to write about! And, of course, you for buying this book!

Introduction

Define the word 'great'. We have taken note of some definitions that the dictionary provides us with:

Remarkable or outstanding in magnitude, degree or extent
Superior in quality or character; noble
Of outstanding significance or importance

There have been many people who have passed through the doors of the Vetch Field in the club's history who have served the club with pride, passion and more importantly excellence. Be it through their goal-scoring records, defensive duties or just plain footballing ability, they are the people that we remember with fond memories of our own of what they have brought to the football club. But we don't stop at players. We also remember the managers that have brought success to the club through their own skills. No-one can ever forget what people like John Toshack, Frank Burrows and even John Hollins brought to this football club during their time in the manager's office. On the playing side the names of Robbie James, Ivor Allchurch, Alan Curtis and Roger Freestone are inscribed in the memories of every Swansea City fan.

I still remember the day that I started supporting the Swans. It was back in the late 1970s and it was an introduction by my brother. Over the past twenty-five years I have cursed him for that at times but at the same time I wouldn't have it any other way. To me this is no ordinary football club. I have seen us at the very top of the football league ladder and, sadly, at the very bottom of the same scale. I have been lucky enough to see us play twice at Wembley and I will never forget the day back in 1985 when the club I love almost ceased to exist. I can assure you that there are not too many football fans who can say that they have seen their club do all that in just one lifetime.

During that same period I think of the players that I have seen pull on the black-and-white shirt. Toshack, James, Charles, Hadziabdic and Hutchison – I could go on for a long time on this subject but I think you are catching the drift. Of course, as with any club, there are players that I would rather forget, people that are probably as far from a book on greats as you can possibly get. But if it wasn't for them then we wouldn't have anything to talk about, would we?

In this book, Keith and I have looked back over the ninety years that Swansea City has existed. We have narrowed a list down from over 800 names to just 100. There are names that we have missed out that we could easily have put in. We make no apologies for this. There are no criteria that we worked with, just people that we think have given something to the club and that it is something that we remember be they Championship-winning players, natural goal-scorers or international players. As you read through this book we expect you to say 'he shouldn't be in there' and you will argue the case for someone that isn't here, but that is football and it is about opinions. We have taken others' opinions and we have narrowed the list down from there.

With each entry in the book we have included a short history of their career together with details of how many league appearances they made for the Swans and how many times they found the net. Thanks to Colin Jones we have a picture of most of them and the years in which they played for the club. In short it is 100 Swansea Greats in words, pictures and statistics. There is no ranking in the 100 people in here and because of this, and to avoid arguments, they are listed in alphabetical order. I am sure that every one of you will have your own thoughts as to who is the greatest of all, although the name of Ivor Allchurch will come very high on that list and that will be one of the reasons why they are looking to erect his statue outside the new stadium.

This, as I have said before, is no ordinary football club and as a Swansea fan reading this you should be proud of your team. There is no shame in supporting your local side and it is safe to say that you know all about the highs and lows that this can bring. At the same time you have a passion that is difficult to equal. I know I am proud to be a Jack and so should you be.

I hope you enjoy this book as much as we have enjoyed putting it together. I will happily admit that there are players in here I knew nothing about before we started, but now I feel as if I actually saw them all play! We present for you, quite simply, 100 Swansea Greats.

Phil Sumbler

Note on the statistics

The statistics given for each player at the start of their profile refer purely to league games where as in the text we refer to league and cup games in some profiles. Unfortunately we were unable to obtain cup records for every player in the book and decided in the interests of balanced reporting we should just include league stats at the start of profiles. However, we make no apologies for referring to cup games in the text of the more recent players in the list.

100 Swansea City Greats

Ivor Allchurch
Len Allchurch
Billy Ball
Tommy Bamford
Danny Bartley
Cyril Beech
Gilbert Beech
Phil Boersma
W.Y. Brown
Ron Burgess
Frank Burns
Frank Burrows
Ian Callaghan
Jeremy Charles
Mel Charles
Chris Coleman
Jimmy Collins
John Cornforth
Tommy Craig
Alan Curtis
Nick Cusack
Alan Davies
Dai Davies
Willie Davies
Harry Deacon
Noel Dwyer
Brian Evans
Roy Evans
Wyndham Evans
Alex Ferguson
Trevor Ford
Jack Fowler
Roger Freestone
Jimmy Gilligan

Vic Gomersall
Harry Griffiths
Dave Gwyther
Dzemal Hadziabdic
Harry Hanford
Billy Hole
John Hollins
David Hough
Brian Hughes
Mike Hughes
Tommy Hutchison
Leighton James
Robbie James
Mike Johnson
Cliff Jones
Ivor Jones
Rory Keane
Tom Kiley
John King
Bob Latchford
Sid Lawrence
Andrew Legg
Dudley Lewis
Wilf Lewis
Billy Lucas
John Mahoney
Chris Marustik
Billy McCandless
Sean McCarthy
Jimmy McLaughlin
Lachlan McPherson
Terry Medwin
Andrew Melville
Tony Millington

Wilf Milne
Jan Molby
Trevor Morris
Dai Nicholas
Mel Nurse
Jack O'Driscoll
Colin Pascoe
Roy Paul
Cyril Pearce
Terry Phelan
Leighton Phillips
Ante Rajkovic
Brayley Reynolds
Stan Richards
Jimmy Rimmer
Neil Robinson
William (Billy) Screen
Frank Scrine
Tommy Smith
Nigel Stevenson
Joe Sykes
Geoff Thomas
Len Thompson
John Toshack
Lee Trundle
Alan Waddle
Keith Walker
Reg Weston
Walter Whittaker
Herbie Williams
Ronnie Williams
Arthur Willis

The twenty who appear here in italics have longer entries

Ivor Allchurch
1949-1958, 1965-1968

League Appearances 445   League Goals 164

There was never any doubt that the name of Ivor Allchurch was to feature in this book. Ivor was one of the greatest Welsh-born players to ever grace a football pitch and it was back in 1949 that he made his debut for the Swans in a game against Cardiff City on Christmas Eve. From those early beginnings, Ivor soon established himself in the Swansea side and, just eleven months after making his debut, he was capped by Wales when they played England at Roker Park.

Allchurch though took a few years to catch the eyes of scouts elsewhere and this started when he nabbed a hat-trick (the first of eight for the Swans) against Brentford. Further hat-tricks soon followed in various games and his goals led to him becoming one of the first names on the team sheet when a Welsh side was named. Indeed, Allchurch headed off to Sweden with the Welsh squad for the 1958 World Cup Finals and played a big part in the Welsh march to the quarter-finals' where eventual winners Brazil beat them. His performances in Sweden meant that Swansea were to be hard-pushed to keep hold of their prize asset and £27,000 of Geordie money persuaded them to part with him.

One goal every three games made Allchurch a hit at St James' Park before an £18,000 move back to South Wales – this time at Ninian Park and Cardiff City. But whatever the club, the legend lived on as he spent two seasons as top scorer for the Bluebirds. Most disappointing of all for Swansea fans was watching Ivor notch a hat-trick as Cardiff destroyed the Swans 5-0. The rivalry in those days was hardly comparable with today.

However, the lure of home proved too much for Allchurch and he moved back to the Vetch in 1966, the same year that he was awarded the MBE by the Queen for his services to football. Even at the age of thirty-eight Allchurch could terrorise a defence and he finished his career as the leading Swans scorer of 1967/68 with 21 goals. His Swansea career ended with 166 goals in 446 appearances – a remarkable record for a remarkable man.

Ivor finished matters at Haverfordwest's Bridge Meadow ground and passed away in May 1997. Such was the impact of Ivor on Swansea fans that, at the time of writing this book, fundraising was taking place for a statue of the great man outside the new stadium, ensuring that his legend lives on for many generations to come.

Len Allchurch
1950-1961, 1965-1971

League Appearances 347   League Goals 60

Ivor's younger brother soon followed him into Swansea City Football Club, making his debut shortly before setting off to undertake his two years' national service with the army. Just two years later he again joined Ivor – this time in the Welsh side – when he appeared against Northern Ireland in Belfast. During the course of the 1959/60 season, Allchurch was part of the youngest ever Swansea side that lined up in a league game, with an average age of twenty-one. Allchurch was one of the elder generation of the side, being second eldest at just twenty-six! At the end of the following season, Len was awarded a benefit of £1,000 for ten years' service with the club.

However, like Ivor he was also destined for a move away from the Vetch and he too was moving north, but not quite as far. He moved to Sheffield United for the total of £18,000. Swansea manager Trevor Morris did not want to part with Allchurch but stated after the sale that he had to balance the budget. That may have been the case, but it did not make it any easier for the supporters to stomach. One of their heroes had gone.

His influence quickly rubbed off at Bramall Lane and his first season ended with the side celebrating promotion to the First Division. However, Allchurch returned to Swansea via Stockport County (and the Fourth Division Championship) in 1968, and he took his total goal tally to 60 in 342 games for the club. He retired at the end of the 1970/71 season and moved to Haverfordwest, where he linked up again with his brother.

Billy Ball
1912-1920

League Appearances   57   **League Goals**   27

When you think back over the years that the Swans have been in existence you will remember many players who had more than a keen eye for goal. But few will remember as far back as Billy Ball, who was the first notable scorer that the club had soon after formation in 1912. Ball had been one of the first signings made by manager Walter Whittaker, when he brought him to Swansea from Stoke.

Indeed, Billy's name is etched in the record books at the Vetch as the man who got the very first goal that the club scored in competitive football. Appropriately, this was scored against local rivals Cardiff City in a 1-1 draw.

However, Billy wasn't satisfied with just that as a first, although he would have been less proud to have also been the first Swansea player to be sent off in a competitive match. Hat-tricks bring match balls but that was not a feat that Ball achieved, although he did receive an overcoat from Stewarts, a local firm of tailors, for being the first player to score two goals in a home league match, against Pontypridd in December 1912.

Ball was again on target twice in the semi-final of the Welsh Cup as the Swans defeated Cardiff 4-2 and at the end of the season, with both the Welsh Cup and the Welsh League title in the trophy room at Swansea, it was Ball who was hailed as one of the main reasons behind the club's fantastic start to professional football.

Billy Ball died in his Swansea home in November 1960, aged seventy-two.

Tommy Bamford
1938-1939

League Appearances 36 **League Goals** 14

Tommy Bamford had already had short spells at Cardiff Docks XI, Cardiff Wednesday and Bridgend when he moved to north Wales and joined Wrexham in April 1929. He began as he meant to go on for the Racecourse outfit, scoring on his debut against Accrington Stanley. He had scored 6 times in his opening 7 games and it became clear that Wrexham had signed a great player who was to achieve great things. Bamford certainly stood out in Wrexham in more ways than one; he was one of the few people to have a car in the north Wales town! His goals helped Wrexham to fourth place in the Third Division (North) in 1930/31 and second place in 1932/33. Sadly for the side, it was only the Champions that got promoted at the end of each season.

His goal-scoring feats monopolise the Wrexham record books. He was top scorer in each of the five full seasons that he played for the Robins and in 1933/34 notched an incredible 50 goals – a club record that still stands to this day. He managed to hit hat-tricks on fifteen separate occasions – more than anyone else has managed for the club. On five of those occasions he scored more than three in a game and notched five in the club's biggest win, 11-1 against New Brighton.

Unsurprisingly, Bamford's feats drew the attention of other clubs and in 1934 he was on his way to Old Trafford to play for Manchester United. He proved there that his goals were no fluke as he notched 53 goals in 98 league appearances, including one on his debut against Newcastle.

It was quite a coup when Swans manager Neil Harris signed Bamford and for Tommy it was a move back home – he was born in Port Talbot. Although he was only to play one season for the Swans, he still managed 14 goals in 36 league appearances before the effects of the Second World War kicked in.

During the war he guested for both Hartlepool and Wrexham and the goals kept coming. Bamford to this day still holds numerous Wrexham scoring records, including highest-ever scorer and fastest man to 100 goals – all records that will take some beating.

Bamford died in Wrexham in 1967.

Danny Bartley
1973-1980

League Appearances 199 **League Goals** 8

Danny Bartley started his professional career at Ashton Gate, Bristol when already an England Youth international. His league debut came in December 1965 when he lined up for the Robins against Wolverhampton Wanderers. He did struggle to hold down a regular place in the side and, after just 101 league games in almost eight years, he left the club along with Dave Bruton to join Swansea for £10,000. He had managed 8 goals during that period.

The following season the Swans were struggling on the pitch and were slipping towards the bottom of the Fourth Division. In desperation, Harry Griffiths was trying varied combinations of his team. One of them was to try Bartley in a left full-back role with Wyndham Evans as his opposite number. While the move worked out, it did not stop the Swans finishing bottom of the Fourth Division and, for the first time in their history, they had to apply for re-election to the Football League.

Of course that re-election appeal was won and, in 1976/77, Bartley was one of only twenty players that Harry Griffiths used as the club narrowly missed out on promotion to the Third Division and his partnership with Evans was going from strength to strength. Bartley again played his part the following season as the Swans won promotion to the Third Division, and he was a major part of the second consecutive promotion that followed the next season. Indeed, with the Swans needing to win against Chesterfield to gain promotion it was Bartley who floated a perfect cross that was met by the head of John Toshack to seal the feat.

As Toshack prepared his side for the Second Division there were several new faces arriving, but Bartley held his place in the side and helped them into a respectable mid-table position. However, with the arrival of Dzemal Hadziabdic his appearances were to be limited and he was given a free transfer to allow him to join Hereford United. He had proved himself to be a very popular player at the club and no-one begrudged him his move – all were appreciative of the work he had done through some of the club's darkest years. In total he had played 199 League games for the club, finding the net on 8 occasions.

After leaving Hereford he moved into non-league football and made appearances for Trowbridge Town, Forest Green Rovers, Maesteg Park, Port Talbot and Bridgend Town.

Cyril Beech
1949-1954

League Appearances 136 **League Goals** 29

Cyril Beech joined Swansea from Merthyr Tydfil at the same time as his older brother Gilbert when he signed in 1949. The Swans were still victorious from the Championship side of the season before but Cyril was one of just three signings that manager Billy McCandless made as he looked to build on that Championship success. Beech though had to wait until the end of that year for his debut as McCandless stuck more or less with the same side that had served him so well the year before. However, he introduced Beech towards the end of December, when the club looked safe from relegation, to give him his debut.

Cyril was a winger who was very pacy and this soon earned him the nickname 'Tulyar' (after the famous racehorse). Unsurprisingly for a winger, Beech set up many goals during his six years at the club with his runs down the wing and crosses from the dead-ball line. However, it was not just his ability to create goals that allowed Cyril to create a name for himself, but also his own eye for goal – he averaged one goal every four games for the Swans.

During the course of the 1952/53 season, the Beech brothers were one of three sets of brothers used by the Swans – Ivor and Len Allchurch and Bryn and Cliff Jones being the others. It is safe to say that this is a record that is unlikely ever to be matched.

After six years at the club, in 1955 he left to join non-league Worcester City, where he played for two seasons. However, after that period he was back in the Football League and Wales when he signed on the dotted line for Newport County. He played 39 games in total for the Somerton Park side, scoring on 8 occasions, before hanging up his boots for the last time.

Beech died in November 2001.

Gilbert Beech
1949-1957

League Appearances   157   **League Goals**   3

Gilbert Beech started his footballing career with Walsall, where he played for two years before moving to play for Birmingham in the Works Association. His performances for the Midlands side soon caught the eye of the Merthyr manager Albert Lyndon, who invited him for a trial. It only took a few games for Beech to impress the side and he turned professional for the club: he was soon joined by his younger brother, Cyril. As the Swans were on the way to the Third Division Championship in 1949 they managed to reach the Welsh Cup final, where their opponents were Merthyr and the Beech brothers. It was Gilbert who caught the eye as Merthyr ran out 2-0 winners in the game at Ninian Park, and that was enough to persuade Billy McCandless to make an offer for him.

Beech was joined at Swansea by Cyril but McCandless preferred to start the season with the side that had served him so well the term before and it was almost the end of the year before Gilbert was pitched in for his first-team debut.

During the course of Beech's ten years at the club he managed to ensure that they stayed a Second Division club in the days when Beech was very much one of the 'odd ones out' for being English. Most of the Swansea squad at this stage was not only Welsh, but also born and bred in Swansea, making their feats all the more remarkable.

Beech went on to play in 157 league games for the Swans, scoring twice in his ten years at the club and, although never able to establish himself as an automatic choice he was an important part of the team in the 1950s and showed great loyalty to the club.

Phil Boersma
1978-1979

| League Appearances | 18 | League Goals | 1 |

You may question the addition of someone in this book who only made 18 League appearances for the club but Phil Boersma was as much a part of the management team that took us to the giddy heights of the early 1980s as John Toshack was.

Boersma arrived at the Vetch in September 1978 when Toshack paid a then-club-record fee of £35,000 to Luton Town to get his man. It was a stage that was odd for long-suffering Swansea fans, who were also aware that Toshack was after Liverpool legend Ian Callaghan at the time. The fans had been more used to seeing their best players leaving but now Toshack was giving them a new concept of keeping the best players and adding players of equal quality to them. Toshack had made a fantastic difference to Swansea and by the time Boersma made his debut the club were top of the Third Division and Toshack had a Manager of the Month award under his belt.

With around a month of the season to go, Boersma was named in the squad that travelled to the County Ground, Swindon for a League match. Swindon were challenging for promotion along with the Swans and as expected it was a keenly challenged contest. Sadly for Boersma, he was clattered by a heavy challenge from Mark Aizlewood of Swindon and he was stretchered off the pitch. It was later announced that Boersma would have to retire from playing competitive football. However, Boersma remained on the coaching staff at the Vetch and was there on the day that sealed the Swans' promotion to the First Division, although there must have been a thought at the back of his mind that he could well have been on the pitch that day had fate not played that little card.

Boersma was promoted to assistant manager of the Swans at the start of the 1981/82 season and his first game in that position was, of course, the 5-1 rout of Leeds United at the Vetch. For a player who had seen his career cut short by that ankle injury sustained at Swindon it was fitting that he was still part of the Swansea set-up in their most historic season. Boersma has also been on the coaching staff at both Blackburn Rovers and Newcastle United under Graeme Souness.

W.Y. Brown
1920-1922

| League Appearances | 65 | League Goals | 16 |

It seems a strange managerial decision to make a signing, as the Swans did in 1919/20, to rectify a goal-scoring problem and then put that solution in at centre half. However, that is what they did when they made the signing of W.Y. Brown.

It was against Cardiff City that he made his debut in that position, much to the confusion of the watching public, but, by the end of the season, he had moved to centre forward to form a striking partnership with Ivor Jones. As the Swans entered the Football League in the 1920/21 season, Brown was made the club's first League captain and his form over that season started the rumours that he was about to call it a day and retire. However, Brown carried on and the following season he notched up a Swansea first, along with Jimmy Collins, when both players notched a hat-trick in an 8-1 demolition of Bristol Rovers at the Vetch Field. The game was all the more remarkable when you consider that in the eleven games preceding the Rovers one, the Swans had only managed eight goals!

Brown died on 1 April 1963.

Ron Burgess
1954-1956, Manager 1955-1957

| League Appearances | 46 | League Goals | 1 |

Ron Burgess started his career at Spurs in May 1936 as a forward. Just twelve months later Spurs were ready to release him from the club but called him up for an 'A' team game as a late replacement. He shone in that game and Spurs changed their mind about releasing him. They offered him a place on the ground staff and an amateur contract at the club. Eventually he won himself a regular spot in the first team and within nine months of his debut for the club he was capped for his country. Not bad for a person who was close to being thrown on the football scrapheap.

As the Second World War dawned the Football League was scrapped for a while but Burgess continued to play the game and won representative honours for the RAF, FA and his country and, when he got the chance, still turned out for Spurs and guested occasionally for Notts County.

When the war ended, he moved full-back positions at White Hart Lane and became a left-back. He captained Spurs for eight consecutive seasons. It was during his term of captaincy that Spurs won the Second and First Division Championships in consecutive seasons and he was also appointed as captain of Wales. In total he won 32 caps for Wales and also gained the distinction of being the first Welshman to represent the Football League. In 1947 he also played for Great Britain against the Rest of Europe in a competitive game. He made his last competitive appearance for Wales in

Ron Burgess in action.

May 1954 and, shortly after, was given a free transfer by Spurs to enable him to join Swansea in a player-coach capacity. He made an instant impact on his debut when the Swans beat West Ham 5-2 at the Vetch in the opening game of the 1954/55 season.

The club was saddened at the start of the 1955/56 season when manager Billy McCandless died. As the club struggled to come to terms with their grief the directors decided that Billy would not be replaced in the short term. They appointed Burgess as team manager and created a committee of three for team selection. Burgess opted not to select himself that often and as the season reached the fifteen-game mark, the Swans had won ten, drawn two and Burgess had appeared just once. The performances slipped away that season and the club finished a respectable tenth, but it could have been so much better.

Burgess used his Tottenham influence in the summer of 1956 when he brought former Spurs player Derek King to the club. Further signings followed in Mal Morris and Derek Blackburn, who both failed to settle. However, the finger of blame was not pointed at Burgess, more towards the policies that the board had put forward in restricting the money that Burgess could spend. However, his influence was still rubbing off and the team yet again finished tenth at the end of his second season.

As the 1957/58 season dawned, fans were still critical of the board but Burgess claimed that he had the players to lead the club into the First Division. An opening day 5-1 hammering of Lincoln City seemed to back this up, and even a 4-4 draw in the second game did not dampen the optimism. However, the side soon started to struggle and further criticism came when Burgess was denied the £20,000 he wanted to bring Ray Daniel to the Vetch. By the end of November the side was bottom of the League and Burgess had to use all his powers of persuasion to get Mel Charles and Johnny King to stay at the club. Even when he was given permission to spend some money he found it difficult to attract players to a struggling club and Burgess became frustrated in his efforts. However, Swansea pulled off a miracle escape and seven points from the last eight saw them just avoid relegation, much to the relief of all the supporters.

In the close season Swansea appointed Trevor Morris as general manager of the club to look after the day-to-day running, but Burgess was not happy and, by the end of August, he had resigned from the club – unprepared to take on a role as effectively assistant manager. Burgess moved on to Watford as manager when he left Swansea, and it was there that he discovered a young goalkeeper by the name of Pat Jennings – who he eventually transferred to his old club Tottenham Hotspur.

Burgess died on 14 February 2005.

Frank Burns
1946-1952

League Appearances | 171 | League Goals | 8

It is no surprise when you come to a book that is entitled 'Greats' to find so many players from one era, and Frank was another one of those that won a Championship medal in 1948/49. However, he is slightly different from most of his teammates when you consider that only two players from that side didn't receive international recognition. Frank was one of them.

Born in Workington, Frank began his career as an amateur with Wolverhampton but moved to Swansea in the summer of 1944. League football resumed after the Second World War in 1946/47 and Frank made his mark immediately, becoming an ever-present in the Swansea side that season. Being part of the defence that was so solid during the Championship season it is surprising when you think of the fact that he was never looked at for international recognition – maybe being an Englishman playing in the Third Division did not help his cause on that front?

Three more seasons followed at the Vetch after that Championship season for Frank before the Swans let him leave to join Southend in the summer of 1952. In total he had made more than 170 appearances for the club, scoring 9 goals. A further 118 appearances followed in spells at Roots Hall and also at Crewe before he called a halt to his professional career.

Frank Burrows
Manager 1991-1995

Frank Burrows began his career as a player back in his native Scotland with Raith Rovers before Scunthorpe United persuaded him to move south of the border and join them in 1965. A total of 106 league appearances in the next three years followed before he moved on to Swindon Town in 1968 for the sum of £12,000.

Twelve months later Burrows was part of the proudest day in Swindon's history when, as a Third Division club, they made the League Cup final and Arsenal beckoned at Wembley. Being heavy underdogs for the day meant nothing to Swindon when they triumphed 3-1 on 15 March. Promotion followed later on that season and Burrows' performances in the Swindon defence played no small part in that success.

Seven more seasons followed at Swindon before he hung up his boots and moved onto the management ladder as assistant manager of the club he had served so well. Burrows was switching between coaching and management in his first days after quitting playing and, after a spell as coach of Swindon, he moved to Portsmouth in 1978 where he eventually succeeded Jimmy Dickinson as the manager. Burrows' first success in management came at Fratton Park as they won promotion from the Fourth Division in his first season in charge.

In 1982, he moved to local rivals Southampton as coach before taking a similar role at Sunderland. However, the lure of management was too much and, in 1986, Burrows worked his way into south Wales where he took charge at Cardiff City as they were relegated to the Fourth Division for the first time in their history. Two years later he reversed Cardiff's league position as they finished as runners-up, but was straight on the move again to take over the assistant's post at Portsmouth. When John Gregory left the club, Burrows was back in charge for a second time before joining Swansea in March 1991.

Burrows was quick to strengthen the side that he inherited and Swansea immediately picked up the Welsh Cup with a triumph over Wrexham in Cardiff. A Rumbelows Cup victory over Tottenham followed the next season, as did a two-legged battle with Monaco in the European Cup Winners' Cup. Burrows was laying the foundations of a very decent Swansea side and the following season he came so close to taking them into Division One. A late surge saw the Swans end up in the play-offs and a two-legged affair with West Bromwich Albion that they narrowly lost 3-2, and hopes were high around Swansea that they could put the run together the next year.

Although they failed to match their league form in 1993/94 Burrows gained the distinction of becoming the first Swansea manager to lead his team to Wembley when they reached the Autoglass Trophy final after a two-legged Southern Area final victory over Wycombe Wanderers. Twenty thousand Swansea fans followed Burrows and his team up the M4 and the delight on his face was clear to see as Swansea lifted the trophy on penalties after a 1-1 draw against Huddersfield Town. Burrows had shaped a side full of talent and this was just reward for his management skills.

The following season was an average one for the Swans but the club was struggling on the pitch and Burrows resigned from his post in October 1995, with the side seemingly heading for relegation and a change in ownership imminent. It was a far cry from a few months prior to this when the Swans went on an incredible FA Cup run that saw them knocked out in the fifth round by Newcastle. Kevin Keegan described the side as 'wonderful', and Swans fans were voted the best to visit Tyneside that season. Swansea City were playing total football.

Burrows had a spell at West Ham on the coaching staff before returning to Ninian Park for a second period in charge of Cardiff in 1998, leading them into the Second Division the following season. He is presently on the staff at West Bromwich Albion, having recovered from a life-threatening illness in the last couple of years. Burrows left West Bromwich Albion in 2004 when Bryan Robson was appointed as manager and brought with him his own coaching staff. Frank still scouts for several clubs and lives in Bromsgrove.

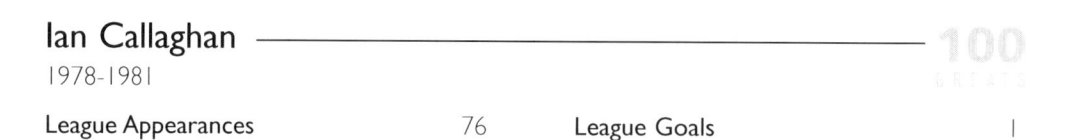

Ian Callaghan
1978-1981

League Appearances 76 **League Goals** 1

Ian Callaghan spent over twenty years of his career at Liverpool, having joined the ground staff at the club in 1957 and making his debut for the first team against Rotherham in April 1960. Callaghan began his early career at Liverpool as an outside right but was soon converted into a midfielder. He was in the Liverpool side that were so famously beaten by Swansea 2-1 in the FA Cup quarter-final of 1964.

Callaghan's name is etched into the record books at Anfield – during his twenty-one-year association with the club he played in a total of 843 games, of which 636 were in the League. He was in the England squad that played (and won) the 1966 World Cup. He also holds an England record of eleven years between successive caps – he won two in 1966 before having to wait a further eleven years until he was picked again.

His roll of honour at Liverpool includes European Cup, League Championship and FA Cup winners' medals and, of course, he appeared alongside John Toshack during the Liverpool glory years of the 1970s. He was awarded the MBE for his services to football as well as being named as the Football Writers' Player of the Year in 1974.

As Toshack departed Anfield for Swansea he quickly gained a reputation for managing to persuade some of his ex-teammates to follow him. Callaghan was one of the first to make that move and, on 2 September 1978, while thinking over the move, Callaghan sat in the stands at the Vetch as his potential new employers went top of the Third Division. Callaghan was also considering an offer from Queens Park Rangers but Toshack's powers of persuasion were the greater and Callaghan dropped down two divisions to join Swansea. He made his debut in a 4-3 win over Tranmere and, by the end of that first season, Callaghan had been very influential in helping the Swans win promotion to the Second Division. It appeared that he had made the right choice in Swansea.

Early in 1980, Callaghan went on to set a new record. With the Swans having disposed of Crystal Palace in the FA Cup after three attempts, Callaghan equalled the record of Sir Stanley Matthews when he appeared in his eighty-fifth FA Cup match, against Reading at the Vetch – a game that the Swans won 4-1. Matthews' record was beaten in the fifth round as Swansea went out 2-0 at West Ham. This statistic is testament to the abilities of the player, considering Liverpool could only compete in a maximum of six FA Cup rounds in any one season.

Callaghan retired from football at the end of the 1979/80 season but, during his two years at Swansea, he had endeared himself to the fans with the way that he always gave 100 per cent to the club. There were games when you would swear that Callaghan was everywhere and, despite his age creeping up and overtaking him, he was still a match for most players.

In total Ian played 76 League games for the Swans' scoring just once, against Charlton Athletic during December 1979. Ian now occasionally commentates on Radio Five Live.

Jeremy Charles
1976-1983

| League Appearances | 242 | League Goals | 53 |

It should come as no surprise when your father is Mel Charles and your uncle is the legendary John Charles that you become a professional footballer, and that is exactly what happened to the last of the Charles family to play for Swansea.

Jeremy Charles was just sixteen when he made his debut for Swansea and his first goals for the club came in a 4-1 victory over Newport County in the League Cup – two goals made all the more remarkable when you consider that Charles was only a substitute in that game. That was in the 1976/77 season and Charles ended that season with 23 goals to his credit.

Along with Robbie James, Alan Curtis and others, Charles was one of the home-grown talents that were so responsible for the Swans rising from the Fourth to the First Division in four seasons. There are not too many players who can say that they played with the same club in all four divisions of the English League but Charles was just one of a handful of people that Swansea had on their books who managed that.

Promotions were achieved with Charles in both 1977/78 and 1978/79 and, on 2 May 1981, Charles played on Swansea's greatest day when they won promotion to the First Division. With the Swans needing to win to guarantee promotion and 2-1 up in the game it was Jeremy who notched the third and final goal that afternoon to seal promotion to the top flight.

Less than four months later, Charles lined up at a sun-baked Vetch as the Swans started their First Division season and it was a dream start for the Swansea lad as he became the first Swansea player to score in that division – ithin ten minutes of the start. That was to be the high point for Jeremy as he struggled with injuries throughout that season, but he had made his mark and Swansea were desperately trying to hang onto their man, refusing any offer that came their way. In fact, Charles was still on the books at the Vetch when the club were relegated in 1983 but hard times were hitting the Swans and eventually they had to bid goodbye to Jeremy in November of that year, when Queens Park Rangers paid £100,000 to secure his services.

It seems quite strange when you look back at the players that left the Vetch around that time that none of them seemed to settle at their new club and were soon on the move again. Charles was no exception and he was soon on the move to Oxford where he matched his Swansea record by helping Oxford into the First Division for the first time in their history. A Wembley cup final also beckoned for Charles – the Milk Cup (League Cup) rather than the FA Cup – before his career was cut short by injury. His last appearance in the league before giving in to the injury was at Highbury, and he left his final mark on the record books by receiving a red card in that game.

Charles returned to Swansea to work on youth development before moving on to Southampton with Malcolm Elias.

Mel Charles
1952-1959

| League Appearances | 233 | League Goals | 66 |

The surname 'Charles' is legendary in Welsh football, and Mel was the younger brother of Welsh legend John Charles. Although never one to scale the dizzy heights of his brother, Mel spent seven years at the Vetch between 1952 and 1959. A total of 69 goals in 233 games followed in a white shirt as well as international honours that started with a cap against Northern Ireland in 1955. Charles' exploits for Swansea made him a certainty as Wales qualified for the 1958 World Cup Finals in Sweden, and he was voted as the best centre half of the tournament during the competition.

Naturally this alerted the top clubs as to his ability and he joined Arsenal the following year for £42,750 as well as David Dodson and Peter Davies going the other way. Charles was a utility player, playing in several positions for both club and country and his Arsenal debut came with him playing at centre half against Sheffield Wednesday. However, a couple of cartilage operations later he found himself as centre forward at the start of the 1961/62 season, making a stunning impact with 11 goals in the first 18 games. However, that was not enough to ensure his place in the side and a move to Cardiff City followed.

An immediate first choice at Ninian Park, he kept his place in the side ironically until his brother returned from Italy and took his place. A spell in the Welsh League followed before he returned to the Football League and Port Vale, where he finished his career and set up his own business in Swansea.

Chris Coleman
1987-1991

| League Appearances | 160 | League Goals | 2 |

Chris Coleman was born in Swansea in June 1970 but signed junior forms at Manchester City. In September 1987 Coleman complained that he was homesick. It didn't take much for Terry Yorath to persuade him to come back to his hometown club and he signed for the Swans.

In his first season at the club he was virtually ever-present as the Swans won promotion via the play-offs (although there was no Wembley final in those days) and he proved himself a more than capable replacement for Terry Phelan at left-back. Coleman linked up well with Tommy Hutchison and the football that was played by the Swans during that season was, at times, a sheer joy to watch.

It was clear from watching Coleman what Manchester City had seen in him and he was quick to establish himself as one of the first names on a Swansea team sheet. In four seasons at the Vetch, Coleman appeared in 160 league games, scoring just twice as well as helping the club to Welsh Cup successes in both 1989 and 1991. However, in 1991 Coleman was on his way out of the Vetch when Crystal Palace paid £375,000 for his services with a percentage of any future sale written into the sale agreement. It was when he was at Selhurst Park that Coleman won the first of his 34 caps for Wales when he appeared against Austria in 1992.

As with Swansea he stayed at Selhurst Park for four years, making 190 appearances for the club and scoring on 14 occasions. Coleman was making an impression and, in December 1995, he was on his way to Blackburn, then Premiership Champions, for £2.8 million, meaning a big windfall for Swansea City and Douglas Sharp. In total the transfer fee received for Coleman stood at just under £1 million, making him the club's record sale.

Coleman was a hit at Ewood Park and, after a shaky start, he established himself alongside Colin Hendry in the centre of the Blackburn defence. Coleman suffered an achilles tendon injury the following season and, when Roy Hodgson was appointed as Blackburn manager, he no longer featured in the plans. Kevin Keegan made his move and paid £2.1 million for Coleman to join his revolution at Craven Cottage. Coleman picked up a Second Division Championship medal in 1998/99. As Fulham were walking away with the First Division Championship in 2000/01, tragedy was to strike Coleman. Driving back home, his Jaguar left the road and collided with a tree. Coleman was lucky not to lose both legs in the accident and tried to fight his way back to fitness. As Fulham celebrated the title in May, Coleman made a poignant appearance on the pitch to lift the trophy, but he was fighting the biggest battle of his career. He made a comeback in March 2002 for Fulham's reserves and also made what was to be his final appearance for Wales as they beat Germany 1-0 in the summer of that year. However, in October he admitted defeat in his comeback and officially retired from playing. He was immediately offered a coaching role at Fulham and also within the Wales set-up and from there he progressed to take over as Fulham manager in 2003, making him the youngest manager in the Premiership at that time.

Jimmy Collins
1919-1930

League Appearances 275 **League Goals** 9

Swansea's scouting back in the early 1920s must have stretched to the army camps as this is where they picked up half-back Jimmy Collins while he was serving in mid-Wales.

As the club struggled to adapt to League football in that period, Collins was tried at many positions during the 1921/22 season in a vain attempt to get the Swans winning. It was during that period that Collins was tried in one game up front and, along with W.Y. Brown, he notched a hat-trick in an 8-1 win over Bristol Rovers at the Vetch. However, in a further 273 league games for the club Collins only managed a further 4 goals – testament to the fact that on that one day he clearly was unstoppable.

By the time he had established himself over the course of the following two seasons, Collins was appointed as club captain at the start of the 1923/24 season. Indeed, he was still captain of the club by the time they won the Third Division (South) Championship the following season, a season in which Collins found himself out of the side on two separate occasions for very differing reasons. Early in the season he suffered a serious injury to his knee that sidelined him for a while and, although he did return during the course of the season, he was suspended later on for a 'serious breach of club discipline' – quite what that breach of discipline was was never revealed.

Towards the end of the 1924/25 season, Collins' popularity as a Swansea player had gone downhill and in one game where he went down with an injury following a heavy tackle, the injury was cheered by sections of the Swansea support, which led to Collins requesting a transfer away from the club immediately after the game had ended. However, he later withdrew that transfer request and carried on in the white shirt, putting in performances that attracted interest from higher-placed clubs.

That interest was never followed up and Collins ended his career where it started, at the Vetch, at the end of the 1929/30 season.

John Cornforth
1991-1996

League Appearances   149   **League Goals**   16

John Cornforth started his career at Sunderland and, after loan spells with Doncaster Rovers, Shrewsbury Town and Lincoln City, he joined the Swans for £50,000 in the summer of 1991. His career at Swansea started slowly due to a broken leg, but it wasn't long after his recovery that he established himself as a regular in the Swans' side and a favourite of the fans at the same time. Cornforth almost helped Swansea back into Division One in 1993 when they agonisingly lost out in the play-offs to West Bromwich Albion over two legs

In 1994, 'Super John' created Swansea history when he was the first captain to lead the club out at Wembley when they qualified for the Autoglass Trophy final. After a 1-1 draw after extra time, Cornforth showed his bottle by stepping forward to take the first penalty – and true to form he scored as Swansea went on to win the shoot-out. Cornforth was the proudest man in the club as he led his side up the famous Wembley steps and lifted the trophy in front of 20,000 of his supporters.

Cornforth was establishing himself as a hero in Swansea and his passing skills were recognised as he was capped in 1995 by Wales when he appeared against both Bulgaria and Georgia. The following season saw John sustain a bad knee injury and it was no surprise that the side slipped down the table without him and were eventually relegated back to Division Three under new manager Jan Molby. Towards the end of that season, Cornforth was sold to Birmingham for a fee of £350,000 to link up with former teammate Jason Bowen. It was not a move that worked out for John and, just a few months later, he was back on the move again, this time to Wycombe. Strangely, when at Birmingham and when in favour with Barry Fry, Cornforth was handed the captain's armband. Despite spending three years at Adams Park he was only able to make 57 appearances for the club and, after a loan spell at Peterborough, he found himself at Swansea's nearest rivals Cardiff on a monthly contract. This was a period in his career he describes as 'my worst'.

A move to Scunthorpe followed in 1999 and a move to Exeter in 2000. The following year Cornforth looked all set for a move back to Swansea but, after a trial at the club, the deal fell through amid rumours of John Hollins, then Swansea manager, not fancying having a crowd favourite back at the Vetch. Corny returned to Exeter and, during the course of the 2001/02 season, he was appointed as manager, moving the club away from the bottom end of the League. The following season, Cornforth was sacked from his position as manager of Exeter and despite being linked twice with a return to the Vetch and the Swansea manager position he accepted a job as manager of Newport County He can still be seen from time to time back at the Vetch in a spectating capacity and whenever there is a managerial change then you can usually guarantee that the name of John Cornforth comes into the reckoning. Cornforth is a Swansea legend cultivated in the 1990s and, with age, definitely a player whose memory will become fonder and fonder as the years go by. When your authors last spoke to John he said to 'Tell the Swansea Jacks I miss them'.

For a man who ended up a journeyman player at the end of his career and could easily have become one from the time he left Sunderland, he found a new home in Wales and married a daughter of the city. In his own words, 'I will come home, when the time is right.' We know he will be made very welcome.

Tommy Craig
1979-1982

| League Appearances | 52 | League Goals | 9 |

John Toshack was a busy man at the start of the 1979/80 season. Shortly after he received a then-club-record £350,000 for Alan Curtis from Leeds United he was quick to go out and spend the money. Part of it was spent on bringing Tommy Craig to the club from Aston Villa. It was a then-club-record fee of £150,000 that Toshack had to pay, the third time in just over twelve months that he had broken the club's transfer record for players in.

Craig didn't take long to pay back some of that outlay, with the Swans looking to build on the back of their two previous promotions. Football was catching the imagination and the average crowd for the season was 14,931 – higher than it had been since the mid-1960s. Much of this was down to the quality of player that Toshack was bringing in and Craig was no exception. With the Swans sitting comfortably in mid-table and a FA Cup run that took them to the fifth round, the foundations were being laid for a promotion challenge the following season. Craig scored twice in a victory over West Ham at the Vetch in March and it was widely recognised that Craig had shown his class in many games over the course of the season.

During the promotion season of 1980/81 Craig found himself out of favour by February with the Swans down in ninth place in the League, fifteen points off leaders West Ham. The Swans had lost five in a row and Toshack was aware that something needed to change, and he turned to old head Craig to inject life back into the side. It worked wonders. In the next match Bolton were beaten at the Vetch 3-0 – thanks to a Leighton James hat-trick – and the Swans were back on course for the greatest day in their history, which was now less than three months away. Craig was on target himself during the Swans' last home game of the season when he scored the second goal to put the Swans 2-0 up, but Luton fought back to secure a 2-2 draw and Swansea went into the last game knowing that a win would secure a place among England's elite.

Backed by 10,000 people, it was Craig who effectively won the Swans promotion when he converted a Neil Robinson cross to put the Swans two up on their way to a 3-1 victory over Preston. Toshack's gamble in bringing back the player had paid dividends and Craig was as happy as any of the home-grown players who had been on this remarkable journey from the start.

Craig left the club at the end of the following season, having been unable to establish himself in a side that had been seriously strengthened for the First Division. However, he had done the job that he was brought in to do and, despite the large sum of money that was spent to secure his services, it was certainly worth it from a results point of view.

Alan Curtis

1972-1979, 1980-1983, 1989-1990

| League Appearances | 358 | League Goals | 95 |

Curt followed his uncle, Roy Paul, into Swansea City Football Club when he left school. A very skilful player, it did not take too long for him to become a Vetch Field favourite after he made his debut in the last game of the 1972/73 season against Charlton. Curt established himself in the team under Harry Griffiths and, by the time Silver Jubilee year arrived in 1977, his was a name that was one of the first on the team sheet each week. He notched his first hat-trick for the club when Newport County were the opposition in the Welsh Cup in that year and the 1976/77 season closed with 14 goals next to the name of Alan Curtis in the Vetch record books.

The following season was arguably Curt's finest in a Swansea shirt as he topped the Fourth Division scoring chart with an incredible 32 goals – a tally that no-one has been able to match. It was an electric year for Swansea as a whole as they won promotion to the Third Division, and it was topped with a club League record 8-0 victory over Hartlepool United at the Vetch. The day was made more special by hat-tricks from both Curt and Robbie James.

After helping the Swans to a second successive promotion in 1978/79, Curt was moving out of the exit door at the Vetch for the first time as he joined Leeds United for £350,000 – a move that never paid dividends for the local lad. Just eighteen months after heading to Yorkshire, he was back for a cut-price £165,000. It was the start of a dream for Curt as just five months later he was part of the Swansea side that was celebrating winning promotion to the top flight for the first, and to date only, time in their history. Thousands of Swansea fans celebrated the day along with Curt and his teammates at Preston as the Swans won 3-1.

As quite often happens in football, fate played a hand for Curt as the fixtures for the following season were announced. The first opponents were to be Leeds at the Vetch and in glorious sunshine it was an Alan Curtis special that rounded off a 5-1 victory for the Swans. That picture of him whirling away after scoring in front of 25,000 Swansea fanatics is a special one, and a Swansea memory that will last forever.

The Swansea dream turned sour after two seasons in the First Division and Curt was on the move again – this time to Southampton. Yet again he failed to settle and, via Stoke City, he returned to South Wales, this time with Cardiff City. The highlight of his time at Ninian Park was the only goal of a Welsh Cup final against Wrexham – ironically at the Vetch. Some Cardiff fans gloat about Curt's time with them, but his heart was and always will be at the Vetch Field.

Swansea City was in his blood and Curt was back at the Vetch again in 1989, calling a halt to an eighteen-year playing career in 1990, having scored just short of 100 League goals. Curt returned to the Vetch for a fourth time on the youth development side before moving up the ranks as assistant manager to John Hollins and, as a team, they won the Third Division Championship in 2000.

It all turned sour just fifteen months after that Championship triumph for Curt as he and Hollins were both sacked after a dismal run of results. A fifth return to the Vetch came early in 2002 and he remained part of the coaching staff at the Vetch until 2005. Alan now works in hospitality at the new stadium. He is a true Swansea legend.

Nick Cusack
1997-2002

| League Appearances | 198 | League Goals | 13 |

Nick Cusack was born in Rotherham on 24 December 1965 and started his career at Alvecurch before moving on to Leicester City in 1987. The spell only lasted for one year before he was on his way again – for £40,000 to Peterborough – before a £100,000 move to Motherwell in 1989. A hard-working midfielder, he found it hard to settle at several clubs and further moves to Darlington, Oxford, Wycombe and Fulham followed before he found himself as one of Alan Cork's signings for Swansea in 1997.

He was soon appointed as club captain although the fans took a while to take to him. He led the side to a FA Cup win over West Ham in 1999 as well as a play-off final before, in one of his proudest moments, he lifted the Third Division Championship trophy at Rotherham in 2000. But still he was far from a crowd favourite, with many people believing that he did not inspire the side the way that a leader should, and there was plenty of criticism of the Championship team during that summer. Cusack's loyalty to Hollins was another matter too. Some fans could not understand why he would stand up for a man who was leading the club to disaster, and time told us all that Cusack's judgement and loyalty here were clouded. It was something he would later suffer from, but that did not stop him wearing his heart on his sleeve.

Immediate relegation followed from the Second Division but it was late in 2001 that Cusack really won the fans over and became a folk hero in Swansea. Following the relegation, the Swans changed hands twice, first to Mike Lewis and then to Tony Petty – a cockney based in Australia. One of the first actions of Tony Petty was to try and immediately terminate the contracts of nine of the playing staff, a move that naturally bought outrage among the supporters. Cusack, the PFA representative at the club and also chairman of the organisation, sprung into action and conducted himself with great credit while the proverbial was hitting the fan around him. In fact, many will say that it was Cusack that kept the playing staff together at the club during the course of the season and that in turn kept us in the Football League.

Cusack was in action again on Christmas Eve, his thirty-sixth birthday, when it was revealed that the players would not be paid for Christmas. Again Cusack was at the forefront of the negotiations and eventually played his part in the club ridding itself of Tony Petty. Under the control of the new ownership things soon changed and, when Colin Addison and Peter Nicholas left the club, it was Cusack, along with Roger Freestone, who was placed in temporary charge of matters. This position was made permanent towards the end of the 2001/02 season. He was given free reign to rebuild the playing squad and brought in nine new faces during the course of the summer, leading many people to believe that Swansea were about to climb back in the right direction. However, the dream was soon to turn sour, not just for Cusack but also for the club as Nick achieved the dubious 'honour' of becoming the first Swansea manager to take the club to the bottom of the Football League. Cusack was sacked from Swansea in September 2002 after a defeat at Boston and took a position at the PFA. However, Richard Jobson replaced him as chairman of the organisation on the basis that the chairman has to be a current player.

Although many will now admit that the appointment of Cusack was a mistake, few will forget the work that he did in the dark days at the end of 2001. Nick remains a member of staff within the PFA

Alan Davies
1987-1989, 1990-1992

| League Appearances | 197 | League Goals | 12 |

Alan Davies began his career at Old Trafford where he made his debut for Manchester United on 1 May 1982 against Southampton – coincidentally at a time when Swansea were up there and competing on a level with the Red Devils. He was quickly bandied about in the press as one of the big stars of the Old Trafford future but, surprisingly, he was never able to establish himself in the first team, competing for places with the likes of Bryan Robson and Norman Whiteside. He did play in the 1983 FA Cup final, where hot favourites United needed a replay to beat Brighton.

A broken ankle soon after that final effectively bought a halt to his career in Manchester and in the summer of 1985 he was on the move to Newcastle United. Again, he was unable to establish himself in the side and loan spells at Charlton and Carlisle followed before Terry Yorath brought him to the Vetch in July 1987. Davies' debut for the club came in the opening day win over Stockport in August 1987 and Davies was a virtual ever-present in the Swans midfield as they won promotion via the play-offs that season. After sneaking into the play-offs on the last day of the season, the midfield combination of Davies and Robbie James were instrumental. After a two-legged semi-final victory over Rotherham, the Swans sealed promotion with a 2-1 win over Torquay at the Vetch before drawing an incredible second leg 3-3 at Plainmoor. Another solid season followed the next year before he was on the move again – this time to Bradford City. He played just one season at Valley Parade before moving back to the Swans in 1990. Davies was capped 11 times by Wales during his career and scored 12 goals in 127 league games for the club.

However, it all ended tragically for Davies when he took his own life in a fume-filled car in February 1992. It was a tragic end for a career that promised so much and Swansea fans had taken to Davies as one of their own – Swansea was the only place where he ever really seemed comfortable playing. It was a very sad end to a professional career that could have offered so much more had Davies been at the Vetch for the Frank Burrows total football revolution that followed.

Dai Davies
1969-1970, 1973, 1981-1983

League Appearances 86 League Goals 0

Dai Davies was born just up the road from Swansea in Ammanford and began his career in local league football before he signed for the Swans, making his league debut against then-Third Division Champions Chesterfield in the final game of the 1969/70 season. The following season he made his first appearance in a game against Preston North End, the first of a nineteen-game unbeaten sequence for the Swans, but in December 1970 he was on his way to Everton, who paid £25,000 for his services.

It was a learning curve for Davies, who spent four seasons as an understudy and returned to the Vetch for a brief loan spell in the middle of that time. When he returned to Goodison Park he found himself making more appearances and, before a move to Wrexham, he played the first of his 52 games for Wales. He made an immediate impact at the Racecourse Ground as Wrexham won the Third Division Championship and, in 1978/79, he helped Wrexham to their best defensive season ever – 42 goals conceded. John Toshack brought Davies back to the Vetch at the end of the 1980/81 season as he prepared for the club's first season in the top flight.

The move drew some criticism from sections of the Swansea squad who felt that Dave Stewart had deserved a chance in the top flight, but Davies battled against the criticism and, at the end of the 1981/82 season was awarded the Chairman's Cup. But there were times when Davies failed to win the fans over, and sections of the Swans support could not take to him.

Davies equalled the then club record during that season when he remained unbeaten for six consecutive matches, starting with a 2-0 win over Liverpool at the Vetch. He remained the club's first-choice goalkeeper during their two seasons in the top flight. In the summer of 1983 he was on his way to Tranmere Rovers as player-coach and a year later retired from playing. However, he was twice persuaded back into the game – first for Bangor when they qualified for Europe in 1985, and for Wrexham during the 1986 Welsh Cup.

Davies now provides co-commentary for BBC Wales Sport in Cardiff.

Willie Davies
1922-1924, 1933-1936

League Appearances 129 League Goals 22

Willie Davies had two spells for the Swans during the 1920s and 1930s. His first stint at the club started when Swansea paid Rhymney 10s 6d for him and tried him in several positions. It was in this spell with the club that Davies won his first Welsh cap in February 1924 when he scored against Scotland in a 2-0 victory. Davies won a Championship medal with the Swans in 1924 when he was forced, due to injury, to stand in for Billy Hole for most of the second half of the season.

Although a favourite at the club, during the summer of 1924 the Swans were finding themselves in financial difficulties and reluctantly agreed to let Davies go to Cardiff City for just £25. Indeed it was this fee that accounted for the Swans only showing a small loss that season of £16, although they did declare that the fee received for Davies was 'substantial!'

Davies was to prove an instant success at Cardiff as he played in their 1925 FA Cup final appearance and scored 19 goals in 98 appearances for the Ninian Park side. However, an illness kept him out of Cardiff's 1927 FA Cup success and a move to Notts County followed soon afterwards.

After the spell with Notts County that yielded 71 appearances, Davies switched Meadow Lane for White Hart Lane and a spell with Tottenham in 1930 and, after appearing 15 times in Spurs' promotion success of 1933, he returned to the Vetch for the second time. His second spell in Swansea colours saw him net 22 times in 131 League games before departing once more, this time for Llanelli Town. In total, Davies was capped 17 times by Wales in his career and once he ended his footballing career he took charge of caretaking at Pontarddulais School.

Harry Deacon
1922-1931

League Appearances 319 **League Goals** 86

Harry Deacon had been at Birmingham City for two years when he was snapped up by the Swans, along with Len Thompson, in the summer of 1922. Born in Sheffield, Deacon's specialised position was inside forward and he proved to be an almost instant hit with the locals who followed the Swans.

Part of the Championship-winning side of 1924/25, Deacon's goals played no small part in that triumph, including a hat-trick in an early season win against Brentford at the Vetch. Although never backed up with any footage, many reports suggested that in a game against Norwich City he took on and beat five opposing players before notching the second goal of that particular win. Deacon was to experience another golden day on 8 November during that season when he managed to find the net on three occasions against Brentford in front of 11,500 fans at the Vetch. Bizarrely though, Deacon was outshone on the day by Len Thompson, who scored the other four in a 7-0 victory. In fact it was Deacon himself who all but sealed the League title that season with a winning goal at Home Park, Plymouth. With the two sides separated by just one point at the top of the table, 30,000 people watched the game and, despite an early Plymouth goal, the reported travelling support of over 5,000 went mad as Deacon struck a free-kick into the net. The game eventually finished 1-1.

Deacon himself holds the distinction of being the first Swansea player to score a goal in the Second Division, South Shields being the opposition, although the goal was in vain as the Swans slipped to a 2-1 defeat in that particular match.

Deacon was awarded a benefit by the club in 1928 and Hearts travelled down from Edinburgh to compete in the game, which took place in front of more than 9,000 spectators.

The following season, in an incredible game at the Vetch, the Swans drew 5-5 with Blackpool, with the name Deacon on the scoresheet four times. His Swans career ended soon after with 88 goals to his credit in 319 competitive appearances.

Deacon eventually left the Vetch in the summer of 1931.

Noel Dwyer
1960-1965

| League Appearances | 140 | League Goals | 0 |

Noel Dwyer began his football career with Ormeau FC back in his native Ireland before he signed professional forms for Wolverhampton Wanderers, who persuaded him to come to England. He spent five years at the club but found first-team appearances very hard to come by and, by the time he left in December 1958, he had made just 5 League appearances. A move to West Ham followed but again he found it hard to make his mark and, in two years, he made 36 League appearances. However, the impression that he made during those infrequent games was enough for him to get his first appearance for the Republic of Ireland when he played against Sweden.

In the summer of 1960 he left Upton Park and moved to Swansea for £3,500, where he was straight into the first team – making his debut on the opening day of the 1960/61 season in a 2-1 defeat at Sunderland. However, it was a struggling Swansea side that Dwyer had joined and, after ten games, the club were bottom of the Second Division. Dwyer was dropped from the side and then shared the goalkeeping duties for a time with Johnny King.

Dwyer though became a folk hero in Swansea during the FA Cup run of 1963/64. In the quarter-final against Liverpool at Anfield he played the game of his life when the side upset all the odds to beat Liverpool 2-1. Dwyer made countless saves, and that must have been on Ronnie Moran's mind when he missed a penalty. As he watched the penalty sail over the bar, Dwyer was said to have 'patted his leprechaun on the head'!

With the Swans just ninety minutes from Wembley, Dwyer was back in goal for the semi-final against Preston and, with the scores locked at 1-1, Dwyer conceded a speculative forty-yard effort to deny the Swans their much-wanted place at Wembley.

The following season, manager Trevor Morris announced that four players were to leave the Vetch. One of these was Dwyer, who joined Plymouth Argyle in the January for £7,500 – £4,000 more than the club had paid for him. After his spell at Home Park, Dwyer moved to Charlton, where he was forced to call a halt to his professional career through injury.

Brian Evans
1963-1973

| League Appearances | 343 | League Goals | 57 |

Brian Evans was an old-fashioned winger. Then-Swansea manager Trevor Morris paid Abergavenny Town £650 for his services in the summer of 1963 and Evans became a Swan. He was to go on to play for the club for ten years – making an incredible 359 league appearances during that period – testament to the way that he managed to keep himself relatively injury-free during the period. The Swans were struggling for most of Brian's early career with the club, with relegations in both 1964/65 and 1966/67. However, by far Evans' most successful season in a Swansea shirt came in 1969/70 when he played a very large part in the side's promotion from the Fourth Division. Evans formed a lethal wing partnership with Len Allchurch on the opposite flank and, all too often, they provided the ammunition for Herbie Williams and David Gwyther to knock the goals in for the side.

One of Evans' biggest strengths was his quickness off the mark and it was this talent, among others, that won him Welsh Under-23 honours as well as the first of his 7 caps for Wales in 1972. The game against Finland came shortly after Evans, along with teammates Tony Millington and Dave Gwyther, toured New Zealand with a side from the FA of Wales.

As the 1970s neared their midway stage, Swans manager Harry Gregg was looking to strengthen his squad but he was told that he had to sell before he could buy. That paved the way for Evans to be sold for £7,000 to Hereford United after scoring 58 goals for the club. Nine more goals followed for Brian in 48 League games for the Bulls before he left the club to play non-league football, where he finished his career. After he gave up the game, he started his own painting and decorating business in Swansea.

Sadly, Brian died in February 2003 while we were starting out on this project.

Roy Evans
1960-1968

| League Appearances | 214 | League Goals | 7 |

Roy Evans arrived at the Vetch at the start of the 1962/63 season and was a virtual ever-present at full-back that season – meaning that he won the first of 3 Welsh Under-23 caps at the end of the season.

At the start of the 1960s the Swans had a very settled side and Evans was very much a part of that team. His abilities at full-back soon made him a club favourite and when Vic Gomersall joined the club in 1966 the two players formed a very competent pairing at the back. Roy did go on to win 1 full cap for Wales when he appeared at Ninian Park against Northern Ireland in the season that saw him star in the Swans' run to the semi-finals of the FA Cup. In total he played over 200 League games for the club before leaving in 1967 to play for Hereford.

Sadly for Swans fans, Roy Evans was tragically killed in a car crash with another former Swan, Brian Purcell, in 1969 when both were playing at Hereford. The news was treated with great sadness and disbelief in Swansea.

Wyndham Evans
1971-1983

| League Appearances | 390 | League Goals | 20 |

Wyndham Evans saw Swansea's glory years from the very early foundations right through to the bitter end when the club faced up to the possibility of extinction. He played his early football in the Carmarthenshire League, where he was spotted by the then-Swansea manager Roy Bentley. Bentley liked what he saw and Evans lined up in a combination fixture for the Swans

33

before progressing into the reserves as a part-time professional under the reserve team manager Roy Saunders, father of Dean.

He made his debut during the course of the 1969/70 season when he appeared against Bristol Rovers and that was enough to persuade those in charge that he deserved a professional contract during the course of the 1970/71 season. The following season Roy Bentley left the club and Harry Gregg was appointed into the manager's hot seat and, as Gregg tinkered to find out what he thought was his best combination, Evans was at one stage during the 1972/73 season tried as a striker. The opponents that day were Rotherham and Evans did not let Gregg down as he scored the first goal in a very rare away win for the Swans.

The following season Wyndham was appointed as club captain – testament to the way that Gregg viewed the youngster – and the foundations were well and truly laid for forthcoming successes. By the time that John Toshack arrived at the Vetch in March 1978, the name of Evans was well established at number two on the team sheet and it was his consistency in that position that helped the Swans to successive promotions from the Fourth and Third Divisions respectively.

Evans found himself out of the side during the course of the 1980/81 season but, as the club's promotion bid looked like falling by the wayside, Toshack turned to one of his most dependable players at the end of February and it was a move that paid immediate dividends as the Swans cruised to a 3-0 demolition of Bolton Wanderers. Evans kept his place in the side from then on and he was in the team that secured promotion to the top flight that magical day in May 1981 at Preston. Many Swans fans will recall Wyndham's awful attempt at singing when the side were promoted to the top flight. From a balcony in the City he sang, and the world cringed. Thankfully he stuck to football!

Evans was in and out of the team the following season before making his top-flight debut against Tottenham Hotspur, and he managed to achieve his boyhood ambition of playing against Manchester United – his 350th League appearance for the club. In reward for his loyalty to the Swans, Evans received a testimonial match against Liverpool at the Vetch in 1982 and, after half retiring from the game, he came back as a player-coach under Toshack before finally calling a halt to fifteen years with the Swans when he retired in 1985.

Evans still lives and works in Llanelli.

Alex Ferguson
1927-1935

| League Appearances | 280 | League Goals | 0 |

Alex Ferguson began his career as a goalkeeper with Gillingham back in the 1920s. The Swansea board were soon alerted to the performances being put in by Ferguson and, in February 1927, he was signed as cover for Jack Denoon, the Swansea goalkeeper of the time. Ferguson, though, was not happy at being an understudy and his performances in the reserves soon saw him promoted to the first team as Denoon was out of favour. At the start of the 1926/27 season Denoon was on his way out of the club with Ferguson the new first choice in the number one shirt.

In his first season as first choice he helped the Swans achieve a sixth-place finish in the Second Division, their second highest pre-war finish and also a league position that they were not able to match again during Ferguson's time at the Vetch. Over the course of the three seasons between 1928/29 and 1930/31, Ferguson appeared in 108 successive League games, another then-club record. However, despite Ferguson's ever-presence in the Swans' goal, the side was struggling and just holding onto their Second Division place. The goals-against column during those seasons was always entering the high sixties or more and more games were being loat rather than won.

Ferguson though continued to keep his place in the Swansea goal and passed 250 League appearances for the club in the mid-1930s. The Swans' performances in the League were taking a step upwards when Ferguson was made available for transfer at the end of the 1935/36 season after a decade as a player with the club.

Trevor Ford
1946-1947

League Appearances 16 League Goals 9

There is little doubt that the name of Trevor Ford was going to appear in this book. Ford was one of those people who was born to play football and was encouraged to do so at a very early age by his father. That resulted in him appearing for Swansea Schoolboys as a full-back.

It is strange to think that Trevor Ford could have appeared in white at a different sport as he was a very talented cricketer but, after taking trials at a few cricket clubs, he decided that football was to be the path that he took. There was still to be another twist in the tale before he actually made his name in his chosen sport.

Ford was serving in the Royal Artillery during the Second World War and looked to get a place in the service team. However, the team already had two full-backs in situ so Ford was played at centre forward and it was there that he was to stay. The Swans finally signed him for their side in 1942 and he quickly made his name as a very capable goalscorer. Forty-one goals were to follow in the 1945/46 season and his first Welsh cap, but also the attentions of the bigger clubs as Swansea realised that they had someone very special on their hands. Indeed, the 1946/47 season was only sixteen games old when Ford moved to Aston Villa.

Ford's career continued to find that it was running far from smoothly and when he wrote a book about illegal payments to players he was suspended. Although this was lifted, he was back under suspension again when it was revealed that Ford himself, among others, accepted these illegal payments when he had a spell at Roker Park with Sunderland. The suspension led to Ford leaving these shores for Holland and, when the ban was lifted, he returned back to Wales and had spells with both Newport County and Romford. A record of 23 goals in 38 appearances for Wales just about sums up the abilities of Trevor Ford – one of Swansea's more famous sons.

Ford sadly died in May 2003.

Jack Fowler
1924-1929

| League Appearances | 167 | League Goals | 102 |

£1,280. Some of the current players at the Vetch earn that much in a few days, Jack Fowler was purchased for that sum of money in March 1924, when he signed for the club from Plymouth Argyle. It was money well spent as Jack went on to become one of the most prolific strikers in Swansea's history. Fowler had caught the eye of Swans manager Joe Bradshaw in a match that season while playing for Plymouth – Fowler scored both goals in a Pilgrims victory. Indeed, it was reported at the time that if it was not for Denoon in the Swansea goal Fowler would have scored several more.

Fowler made his debut against Southend towards the end of that season to the great surprise of the home crowd. It was noted that the directors failed to co-operate with the press to maximise the attendance at the game. Unsurprisingly though, Fowler scored on his debut and received a warm ovation when he left the field at the end of play.

Swansea were at this stage top of the table but then managed just one win in their next seven games – a sequence ended when Fowler scored his first hat-trick for the club in a win over Brentford. The following season saw Fowler notch a club record five goals in a game as Charlton were crushed at the Vetch 6-1, a record that still stands to this day. A further hat-trick came that season against Luton at the Vetch as the Swans pushed for promotion. The most important goal from Fowler that season though had to be the first in the final day 2-1 win over Exeter that won them the Third Division (South) Championship. Fowler had scored 28 goals in that Championship season, a then-club record.

The following season, backed by the crowd's calling of 'Fow-Fow-Fowler', Jack excelled once more and he netted four League hat-tricks as well as one in a 6-3 victory over Stoke in the FA Cup. Further cup goals against Millwall and Arsenal saw the Swans into the semi-finals where they were eventually well beaten by Bolton 3-0.

Swansea started the following season well and another Fowler hat-trick in a 5-2 win over Barnsley cemented an unbeaten start that lasted into September. A further hat-trick at the beginning of October had helped even more and incredibly, by the end of that month, the Swans were second in the League. However, they slipped down the table and ended the season twelfth, although Fowler was still a regular goalscorer.

In November 1928, Fowler scored in the last minute of a 4-0 win over Tottenham. It was his 100th League goal for the club at a ratio of better than one goal every two appearances. His form, though, was falling away but that did not stop the numbness that the supporters felt when he finally left the club.

In total, Jack Fowler played 167 League games for the club and scored an incredible 102 goals in those games. He netted nine League hat-tricks, a record that you wonder if anyone will ever come close to. He was the club's most prolific scorer at that time and, had it not been for his goals in the Championship season, it is safe to say that Swansea would have come a close second.

He won 6 caps for Wales during his career, winning the first and last of them against England.

Roger Freestone
1991-2004

League Appearances   549   League Goals   3

Roger Freestone began his career at his local club Newport County before catching the eye of Chelsea and moving on to Stamford Bridge. A Second Division Championship medal followed before he fell out of favour with the Blues, and a permanent move to Swansea City followed.

His debut for the Swans was an eventful one, with a television being his take-home bonus as he was the Rumbelows Man of the Match in a cup tie against Tottenham – a match that Swansea won by a goal to nil. Roger soon established himself in the Swansea goal and his reputation as one of the best 'keepers outside the top flight of English football was enhanced with every performance. Indeed, in 1992/93 Roger was close to taking Swansea back into Division One (by this time the Premiership had been formed) but they sadly missed out in the play-offs against West Bromwich Albion.

Moving, though, was never on the mind of a goalkeeper who now valued Wales and all he wanted to do was play football. In 1994 he was rewarded with an appearance with the Swans at Wembley. On a sunny April day, the Swans soon found themselves one up against Huddersfield only to see that lead pegged back in the second half. As extra time passed, the game went to penalties and it was Roger's day to shine as he saved the crucial penalty to give Swansea the Autoglass Trophy.

Roger was back at Wembley just three years later when the Swans reached the play-off final against Northampton Town, but this time the trip was to end in heartbreak as Roger was beaten by a last-minute free-kick from John Frain to keep the Swans in Division Three. Two years later, after helping Swansea to an FA Cup victory over West Ham, it was play-off heartbreak again as the Swans missed out in a semi-final against Scunthorpe – but it was just a warm up in reality for the season to follow, in which it was Roger Freestone the record breaker.

Indeed, it was the whole side that were record breakers that season, although Roger was at the heart of a defence that was the meanest in England during 1999/00. Nine matches in a row were won at one stage during the season, and so many games were won 1-0 along the way that Roger was acknowledged everywhere as the best 'keeper in the division. This was also recognised by Wales manager Mark Hughes who called Roger up into the Welsh squad, and he won his one and only cap against Brazil in front of a capacity crowd at the Millennium Stadium. Unfortunately for him and his teammates, Swansea failed to build on that Championship and within twelve months they were enduring a relegation back to Division Three.

Of course, we also remember Roger as a goalscoring goalkeeper. It was in 1995/96 that Swansea players were having problems from the spot and Roger volunteered for the duties. He grabbed his first career goal at Oxford when he successfully converted a penalty, and two more followed before he gave up the duties, but for a goalkeeper to have a career total of 3 in the goals-scored column is no mean feat.

Roger turned down many opportunities to leave the Swans for more money, including most notably Manchester United, and his loyalty in the modern game is to be highly commended. Roger was released from Swansea City at the end of the 2003/04 season, having racked up almost 550 League appearances and, after a brief spell at Newport County, he retired completely from the game and set up his own business in his local area.

Jimmy Gilligan
1990-1993

League Appearances 62 **League Goals** 23

Jimmy Gilligan started his league career at Watford where he progressed through the ranks and won a FA Youth Cup winners' medal when the Hornets beat Manchester United 7-6 on aggregate in the final. He stayed at Vicarage Road for six seasons but was able to make just 27 appearances in that time and, after a loan spell at Lincoln, he joined Grimsby for £100,000. Further moves followed to Swindon and a loan spell at Newport before he moved back to Lincoln in a permanent move. This was where football threw out one of those strange coincidences – Gilligan was part of the Lincoln side that lost their League status in 1987, ironically at the Vetch Field.

After losing League status with Lincoln, Gilligan moved to south Wales and Cardiff City where Frank Burrows paid £17,500 for his services. He was an instant hit at Ninian Park and scored 20 goals in his first season, helping the Bluebirds to promotion from the Third Division in the process. The following season he was top scorer again before following Burrows to Portsmouth late in 1989.

In August 1990, Terry Yorath persuaded him to return to South Wales and Swansea City and, in another touch of irony, he was working for Frank Burrows again when he replaced Yorath in the Vetch Field hot seat. Gilligan was to prove to be the club's first prolific goalscorer since Bob Latchford and he ended his first season at the Vetch with 16 goals to his credit. In recent times the Swans have not had a great goalscorer to boast about. Gilligan was, and could have been so much more.

He ended the 1990/91 season with 24 goals to his credit in all competitions, which included hat-tricks against Wigan in the League and Llanelli in the Welsh Cup. However, Gilligan was beginning to suffer with a painful back injury and during many of his appearances he was forced to play through the pain barrier. The following season he netted a hat-trick in a 3-0 win at Chester on Boxing Day but the back injuries were proving far too painful and at the end of the 1991/92 season he was forced to retire from playing professionally at the age of just twenty-eight. Gilligan was in his prime, and a great loss to the club.

After a break from the game he was appointed as community officer at Watford and two years later found himself as youth team coach at the club – gaining academy status for the centre of excellence. He joined David Platt at Nottingham Forest when he was appointed as reserve team coach, and when Platt joined the England set-up Gilligan followed him with a brief to look at the countries that were forthcoming fixtures for the national side.

In January 2002 he was appointed regional coach with the PFA whilst still working part time on the England Under-21 set up.

Vic Gomersall
1966-1971

League Appearances 178 **League Goals** 6

Vic Gomersall was born in Manchester and began his career at Maine Road with the local side, Manchester City. Slowly he worked his way through the ranks all the way until he made his debut for the club during the 1960/61 season. However City already had an established player in Gomersall's position in Glyn Pardoe and, during five seasons at the club, he managed just 39 games.

It was in August 1966 that Gomersall moved south to join the Swans and he quickly forged a formidable full-back partnership with Roy Evans. It was not a happy start for Gomersall as, just over five months after joining the club, he was part of the Swansea side that found itself on the wrong end of an FA Cup 'giant-killing' when they lost to Nuneaton Borough.

The season 1967/68 saw the Swans play their first ever season in the Fourth Division and they failed to really match the expectations through lacklustre performances and crowds dwindled. A fire at the Vetch did not help matters but Gomersall was one of the shining lights of the season and, at the end of it, with the club in fifteenth place, he was voted as the Player of the Year.

The following season Swansea fared little better but yet again Gomersall was one of the few gaining positive press as the crowds slipped to their lowest levels ever. However, Gomersall was part of an amazing turnaround the following season, which saw the Swans promoted in third place.

Gomersall left the club at the end of the 1969/70 season having made 180 League appearances in four seasons – almost ever present. He left the club and completed his career in non-league football.

39

Harry Griffiths
1949-1964, Manager 1975-1978

| League Appearances | 422 | League Goals | 72 |

It is reasonably safe to say that Harry Griffiths earned and served the title of a 'Swansea legend'. Having earned schoolboy honours for Swansea as soon as the Second World War ended, Griffiths signed professional forms for the club at the age of seventeen. He made his debut for the club in the Championship-winning season of 1948/49 although he had to wait another three years before he was able to establish himself as a regular at the Vetch Field. His debut came when he was on home leave from the Army.

However, once he had established that position he was very difficult to move out of it and very few games saw the name of Griffiths missing from the team sheet over the next eleven seasons. There were only two positions during that spell that Griffiths did not appear in – centre half and goalkeeper – but it is some form of a travesty that he only won 1 full cap for Wales. That came against Northern Ireland in Belfast in 1953, the same game in which Terry Medwin made his international debut.

Griffiths was awarded a testimonial at the end of his playing career with the club when 12,000 people turned up to pay homage to one of their heroes. He made 242 league appearances in a Swansea shirt before he left the club in 1964 to become player-manager at Merthyr. However, Swansea was in his blood and two years later he was back as first-team coach before taking over as manager in 1975 following the resignation of Harry Gregg. Griffiths was said to be 'delighted' at the chance to take charge of a side that had played him in just about every position possible.

As Griffiths encountered his first close season in charge at the Vetch he spent £1,250 on one player but gathered several more on free transfers. As the season passed the halfway stage Griffiths declared that the side was 'making progress' – they were unbeaten at home but had yet to register an away victory. They ended that 1975/76 season in eleventh place, eleven places up on the position that forced them to apply for re-election just twelve months before.

The Swans made a fantastic start to the following season, beating Newport 4-1 in the League Cup. Griffiths could not hide his delight and pointed out that the Swans were among the best-paid teams in the lower divisions. He said that the treatment that they were receiving from the board should make them 'feel part of a going concern'. However, at the end of the season Griffiths had just missed out on leading the Swans to promotion, although he knew that he could look back on the season with considerable pride.

Rumours circulated Swansea in October 1977 that Griffiths had been sacked from his position as manager, although the official statement was that he had resigned. Public support was there in large numbers for Griffiths, but there was little understanding of the actions behind the scenes. Griffiths stayed at the club in an 'acting' capacity and several leading managers refused the Vetch job. However, when the discussions turned to John Toshack he was delighted to take the job – keeping Griffiths on as his assistant.

It was, tragically, to be a short-term appointment for Griffiths. Scunthorpe arrived at the Vetch on 25 April 1978 with the Swans needing to win both their remaining games to secure promotion. There was a large crowd present for the game, all hoping to celebrate another step closer to promotion. However there was to be no celebration as Griffiths collapsed and died while working in the treatment room prior to the game. The news travelled around the ground as the teams came out and the game was played in an atmosphere of muted respect. The Swans won 3-1 and went on to seal the promotion for which Griffiths had worked so hard. Toshack made his solemn promise to Griffiths' memory: 'We shall leave no stone unturned to do him proud.'

In memory of someone who had given so much to Swansea City, the club named the bar behind the centre stand after him and the legend of Harry Griffiths will live on in the club forever.

Dave Gwyther
1967-1973

| League Appearances | 216 | League Goals | 60 |

South Gower FC. Not the most romantic of clubs but one that Dave Gwyther was playing for when the Swans decided his talents could do a job for them in March 1966. It was the right choice as Gwyther played for the club for the next eight seasons, scoring many vital goals during that period.

During the season of 1968/69 only Herbie Williams managed more goals than Gwyther and it was this sort of statistic that made Bristol Rovers offer £8,000 for his services at the end of the season. But Swansea were determined to hold on to their man and refused the offer while Gwyther remained happy to be at the Vetch.

The following season Gwyther celebrated his twenty-first birthday in style as he notched all four goals in a FA Cup win over Oxford City. His scoring exploits were going from strength to strength by this stage and not only did he top the goalscoring charts at the Vetch but also in the Third Division. During this season he notched his one and only League hat-trick as Reading were beaten 5-0 at the Vetch.

By this time, people in two sections of Cardiff had begun to stand up and take notice of Gwyther and he spent the summer of 1971 on tour with the FA of Wales in New Zealand. Those at Ninian Park were also watching closely and the Swans turned down a bid of £20,000 from Cardiff City.

Gwyther played for the club for two more seasons before he moved to The Shay and a spell with Halifax after scoring 59 League goals for the Swans. Further moves for Gwyther included Rotherham, Newport and Crewe before he returned to South Wales to finish his career at Port Talbot Athletic. Gwyther still lives in Swansea.

Dzemal Hadziabdic
1980-1983

| League Appearances | 89 | League Goals | 1 |

Dzemal Hadziabdic's first taste of football in Wales came at Ninian Park in a European Championship qualifier between Wales and Yugoslavia. Hadziabdic did not endear himself to the crowd that day when most of the spectators claim that he dived when under challenge to win a free-kick. However, despite what the crowd thought, there was someone on the Welsh team who was impressed with Hadziabdic's play – John Toshack. It was that day that a mutual respect was built up between the two players that was going to be to Swansea's advantage in years to come.

The Swans were on a pre-season tour of Scotland in 1980 when Hadziabdic's agent approached Toshack and told him that the player was available for transfer. Toshack cast his mind back four years to that European Championship qualifier and arranged for him to play in a friendly match against Tottenham at the Vetch. Hadziabdic played in that game but was not 100 per cent fit due to a cold. He was replaced but was in front of the North Bank when he was called in. Instead of coming off the pitch the traditional way he walked off the pitch in front of the North Bank so he could run round the pitch to the bench. The crowd gave him a standing ovation and Toshack's mind was made up. Hadziabdic later commented that it was the way he was received by the crowd that had helped make his mind up to come to Swansea.

Of course, being a Yugoslav, he needed a work permit and missed the early games of that season but eventually made his competitive debut in a Swans shirt against Arsenal at Highbury on 2 September. He was immediately given the nickname 'Jimmy' because of the difficulty that the Swans players had in pronouncing his first name. The name took off and from that point on everyone at Swansea knew that he was just plain 'Jimmy'

The team started well during the 1980/81 season and quickly found themselves in fourth place but, by the time November came and went, they were slipping slowly down the League table. This turned when Alan Curtis returned to the Vetch in December, the day before Hadziabdic shone in front of the TV cameras as the Swans beat Newcastle at the Vetch 4-0. Hadziabdic gained a liking to the TV cameras and the next time they were back at the Vetch was in April when Chelsea were beaten 3-0 and Jimmy scored his only goal for the Swans, which prompted him to go on a run back to the other end of the pitch with no Swans player able to touch him.

Jimmy played right through that season and was on the pitch when the Swans gained promotion to the top flight at Preston and the £160,000 that was paid for him was money well spent as far as Toshack was concerned. Jimmy found it tough to adjust to life in the top flight of English football though. He struggled in that opening season with a leg injury, which wasn't helped either by a complete loss of confidence as he was unable to find the top of his form.

Jimmy was never able to repeat the feats of his opening season at the Vetch and left the club as they started their slide back down the Football League ladder. Despite his inability to adjust to life at the top few who saw Jimmy play in the black and white will ever forget him. Jimmy had a spell in charge of the Qatar national side at a time when it was well documented they were ahead of Wales in the world rankings.

Harry Hanford
1927-1936

League Appearances   201   League Goals   0

There aren't too many players in Swansea's history that started their careers on the ground staff at the club but Harry Hanford is one. Having graduated into the first team he made his debut for the club at the end of the 1927/28 season and quickly established himself as not only a regular, but also as a popular player with the fans. His performances on the pitch always attracted rumours that he was about to move away from the club and a couple of firm offers were received for his services. However, Hanford was enjoying his time at Swansea and he opted to stay with the club for the time being.

By the time the 1930s dawned, Hanford had been made club captain and was one of the most consistent players in the Swansea side. In 1934, his performances were recognised by his country and he won the first of his 7 Welsh caps when he played against Northern Ireland. Hanford was capped twice more while playing for the Swans but halfway through the 1935/36 season he left the club to join Sheffield Wednesday for a 'substantial fee'. It was history repeating itself as the Swans were struggling financially and the fans were upset that the best players in the club were being sold to balance the books. He had played a total of 200 league games for the Swans but never managed to find the net while at the Vetch. The sale of Hanford upset matters at the Vetch and the fans started to vote with their feet by staying away from home games in their thousands.

During his time at Hillsborough he won 4 more caps for Wales and took his total League appearances to close on 300 before he moved to Exeter City, where he ended his League career.

Billy Hole
1919-1931

| League Appearances | 341 | League Goals | 36 |

Billy Hole was one of the reasons why Jack Fowler scored so many goals. Billy played on the right wing and provided many of the crosses from which Fowler netted, but also managed 40 goals himself in the 341 League games he appeared in wearing the white shirt.

Billy made his debut for the club in October 1919 when he lined up for the Swans against Brighton at the Vetch. At the time he was a part-time professional on just £3 per week and he appeared on the right wing. Towards the end of that season, Hole was being watched by the people who picked the Welsh team and he grabbed two goals in the penultimate game of the season against Brentford in front of 15,000 people.

In April 1921 Hole won the first of his 9 caps for Wales when he lined up against Northern Ireland at the Vetch. Hole achieved two notable feats on that day. Firstly, he was the first Swansea-born player to represent his coountry while playing for his hometown club. Secondly, he was the first player ever to score an international goal at the Vetch Field.

As the Swans made a good start to the 1923/24 season, they started with an unchanged side for the first twelve games. It was in the last of those games that Billy Hole sustained an injury that was to keep him out of the side for the remainder of that season. While it hurt to watch the matches from the sidelines, Hole was to come back with a vengeance the following season. He started his comeback with a reserve appearance, this coming slightly later than had been initially expected. However, he was soon back in the first team and his appearances helped the Swans to their Third Division (South) Championship of that season.

As Hole's career started coming to a close, he decided that it was time to widen his interests. The Swans were still scoring freely with Hole creating much and, in October 1927, he announced that he was opening a confectionery and tobacco shop in the town. Billy Hole left the Vetch in the summer of 1931, having given twelve years' distinguished service to the club. He had made 341 League appearances for the club and was an extremely popular player with the supporters.

Billy Hole had three sons who all played for the club – Alan, Barrie and Colin made almost 100 League appearances between them but never reached the levels of distinction managed by their father. His shop flourished in the town – something that was no surprise as most things that Billy Hole were involved in were a success.

John Hollins
Manager 1998-2001

John Hollins was born into football. His grandfather played the game, as did his father and also three of his brothers. He started his career when he signed youth terms with Chelsea in the summer of 1961 and two years later he was awarded his first professional contract. It was the start of a love affair for Hollins who served Chelsea for twelve seasons. It was during his time with Chelsea that he won his one and only England cap when he played against Spain in 1967. A FA Cup winners' medal followed in 1970 and in 1971 it was agony for John as he was forced to miss the replay of the European Cup Winners' Cup triumph.

Chelsea were relegated in 1973 and Hollins left the club, moving across London to play for Queens Park Rangers. In 1976, Rangers finished as runners-up in the First Division and Hollins stayed for another four years before he headed in another direction across London to play for Arsenal. He was awarded the MBE for his services to football in 1981. The following year he was given a free transfer from Arsenal and returned to Stamford Bridge as player-coach until his retirement from playing. He was appointed as manager in June 1985. It was an appointment that lasted for three years before he resigned when Chelsea appointed Bobby Campbell as coach without his knowledge.

Hollins stayed out of football for seven years before returning to Queens Park Rangers as reserve-team coach in 1995. In 1998 he ventured out of London to take on the managerial role at Swansea. Hollins made an almost immediate impact at Swansea with the side pushing for an eventual play-off position. However, his greatest achievement in the first season came when his side beat Premiership West Ham in the third round of the FA Cup before losing narrowly to Derby in the following round. Play-off heartbreak followed at Scunthorpe but Hollins looked back on his first season with a degree of satisfaction.

If the first season was a success the second was even better as the Swans won the Division Three Championship and in the process boasted the meanest defence in the Football League. The highest point of the season came in January when a Walter Boyd goal gave the side victory over Macclesfield to record a ninth successive League victory – a club record. The triumph was sealed on the last day of the season at Rotherham – a triumph marred by the death of a long-standing Swans fan outside the ground.

Hollins had drawn his critics and they were out in force again as he failed to strengthen the squad for the Second Division and, despite a promising start, the side were relegated by Easter with one of the worst records in their history. If Hollins ever looks back on his time at Swansea he surely will say that he either failed to strengthen the squad because he didn't want to, or that he was used as a political pawn by the powers that were. Either way he will feel he could have done so much better. This was the root cause of the later problems he had with the loyal Swansea support.

The knives were out for Hollins and after a poor start to 2001/02 he was sacked after a defeat at Plymouth Argyle. A spell at Rochdale followed but that did not work out for Hollins, and his last appointment was as an advisor to then-Stockport County manager Carlton Palmer. Hollins occasionally appears as a pundit for for Sky TV.

David Hough
1982-1991

League Appearances 188   League Goals 9

David Hough was born in Crewe but moved to South Wales with his parents when he was a child. He signed as a youth with the club at the start of the 1980s.

It was an exciting time at Swansea, with the first team riding high in the First Division, and the city had the football buzz. Hough was soon in the youth side and in 1982/83, coincidentally the same season that Swansea were relegated from the top flight, he played a regular part in the youth side's Championship victory. The following season, with the First Division team being torn apart, he found himself making his debut in the side on the last day of the season. Sadly for Hough, it was a sad debut as the side crashed 5-0 at Portsmouth as they confirmed that they deserved their second successive relegation.

Hough was to become a regular, generally in the right-back position, but occasionally needed in the centre of defence – both positions that he looked equally comfortable in. After avoiding relegation the following season with a 0-0 draw in the last game, the Swans were relegated back into the basement division in 1986. Two seasons followed in the basement with Hough forming a good relationship with Terry Phelan in the full-back positions. He was a regular as the side won promotion back to the Third Division via the newly introduced play-offs.

Hough, although a defender, loved nothing more than overlapping from full-back and reaching the byline to put in the 'killer' cross, and many Swansea goals were created by this method.

As the Swans established themselves as a decent Second Division side, Hough remained a regular until 1991 when he played his final game against Fulham in September. After 227 League games spanning just over seven seasons he was, at that stage, the longest-serving player on the club's books. After retiring from the game, David joined the South Wales Police where he managed to combine his duties with football action for the Police football team. Keith Haynes has had the pleasure of lining up against Hough in a non-league competitive game in Gloucester in 1992 where Hough worked as tirelessly as ever in his defensive position. David worked his way up to the rank of sergeant in the constabulary. He was probably one of the unsung heroes of the 1980s and was given the tough task of following the best Swansea generation ever. It was a feat that he managed with great dignity and loyalty to the club.

Brian Hughes
1956-1966, 1969

League Appearances   231   League Goals   7

Brian Hughes was signed by the Swans as a youngster and worked his way up through the various stages of the club before progressing into the first team during the 1958/59 season. In the January of that season Hughes was part of history as the side lined up for a game against Fulham at Craven Cottage. The side that had been picked that day contained eleven internationals. Eight players had played a full international while there were three (Hughes included) who had played at youth level. This had surpassed the previous club first of eleven Welsh internationals for a game in December 1957.

Hughes was also part of another piece of Swansea football history. On 26 April 1960, the team were due to entertain Bristol City at the Vetch. The side ran out convincing 6-1 winners, a score that did flatter the Swans but that took nothing away from the fact that it was the youngest Swansea side ever. The average age of the team that day was just twenty-one with seven of the players, Hughes included, Swansea-born.

Early in 1961, with the Swans battling against relegation, Hughes dislocated his shoulder in a 6-2 defeat at Charlton, an injury that kept him out of the game for a while, but he recovered to regain his place in the first team later on that season.

Hughes played a very important part in Swansea's run to the FA Cup semi-finals in 1964. His most impressive performance in that run came in the shock 2-1 victory over Liverpool at Anfield. At the end of that game it was acknowledged that Hughes, along with his defensive colleagues, had defended as if their lives depended on it.

Hughes left the club in January 1969 after 231 league games to play for Atlanta Chiefs in the United States. He had managed 6 goals in those appearances for the club as well and had proved a loyal and dependable servant in his eleven-year association with Swansea City.

Mike Hughes
1983-1988

League Appearances   139   League Goals   0

A quick look at the First Division squad of 1981/82 sees a very young Mike Hughes in the team photo. Learning his trade from the likes of Dave Stewart and Dai Davies was obviously a good grounding for Hughes, who had to wait until the 1984/85 season for his break in the first team.

Of course, by this stage, the Swans' First Division dream was a distant memory. They were back in the Third Division and were looking favourites for a third successive relegation. Jimmy Rimmer was at the club by this stage and, as a League and European Cup winner, he was able to pass on some of his expertise to Hughes.

Hughes was to play a bit part in the 1984/85 season but it was some of his performances that gained valuable points for the Swans as they avoided relegation on the last day of the season. A total of 27 League appearances followed the next season but they were not enough to save Swansea from falling back to the basement division. It was clear, though, that Hughes was a talent that was to be nurtured.

During the course of the 1986/87 season Hughes was ever present in the League and his performances brought rave reviews from those that watched him. He was agile in the air and his shot-stopping ability was second to none. It seemed as if Swansea had bred a player that was destined for great things. As the Swans built a promotion side under Terry Yorath during the course of the 1987/88 season, it was Hughes that formed the final rock of a strong defensive line. Containing Andy Melville and Chris Coleman as well as Alan Knill and David Hough, the Swans were solid and the results backed this up. However, unbeknown to Hughes tragedy was just around the corner.

After playing against Stockport in a 1-1 draw in February 1988, Hughes was referred for a brain scan. He had been complaining of headaches but nonetheless the procedure was thought to be completely routine. Sadly, for both Hughes and the Swans, the results of the scan suggested that Hughes should retire from the game immediately. It was reported that should he receive another blow to the head the consequences could be fatal and with regret Hughes announced his retirement immediately afterwards.

Swansea had lost a big star from their line-up – someone that would have played at a much higher level. His teammates did him proud and won themselves the deserved promotion via the end-of-season play-offs. However, they had to face the future without Hughes – a sad loss to the game and a tragic end to a great career that was just too short.

Mike was awarded a testimonial match against Tottenham in September 1988, after which he moved to London where he became a prison officer.

Tommy Hutchison
1985-1991

League Appearances   173   League Goals   9

Ask any Swansea fan of the mid-1980s who played left wing for the club and they will smile and fondly recall the exploits of Tommy Hutchison who, remarkably, was still playing League football for the club at the age of forty-three!

Tommy started his football career with Alloa but it was Blackpool who first brought him to England when they signed him in 1968. It was quickly apparent that he was worth every penny that they spent on him and it was his 'assists' that resulted in many goals. The Bloomfield Road outfit won promotion to the old First Division in 1970. Blackpool found life tough at the top and after just one season they were relegated. Twelve months later, after another season shining in the Second Division, Hutchison was on his way to Coventry City.

Eight happy years followed for Hutchison, including a very proud day in 1973 when he won the first of 17 caps for Scotland. As Coventry went from strength to strength in the First Division, Hutchison was a big crowd favourite and he managed to find the target 24 times in 314 games over those eight years – a period in which he remained almost injury free. However, it was a particular feat with Manchester City, whom he joined after leaving Coventry, that he is best remembered for outside of Swansea. Under John Bond, 1980/81 was a good season for the Maine Road side – they reached the semi-finals of the League Cup and the FA Cup final against Tottenham Hotspur. While all the attention was on 'Ossie's Dream' – in reference to Osvaldo Ardiles's desire to play at Wembley – it was Hutchison that caught the headlines. During the course of the first half a spectacular diving header from Tommy put City ahead before in the second half he deflected a Glenn Hoddle free-kick into the goal to become the first man to score at both ends in a Wembley cup final.

Twelve months later Hutchison was on the move again – to Hong Kong – but after one season he was back and signing for Burnley before John Bond persuaded him to join him at the Vetch in July 1985 at the age of thirty-seven. His debut for the Swans came on the opening day of the 1985/86 season against Wigan Athletic and, with most people predicting that he may last one, maybe two seasons on the pitch, they were determined to make the most of the enjoyment that he brought. During the course of the 1987/88 season he spent a brief spell on loan at Blackpool but returned to Swansea to help them to win promotion from the Third Division via the newly introduced play-off system.

Spells as player-coach and caretaker manager were also part of his CV at Swansea and as the 1990s dawned Hutchison set the record as the oldest player to play in European competition when he played in a European Cup Winners' Cup tie against Panathinaikos – one of the most exciting European ties that ever graced the Vetch Field. Time never seemed to catch up with Tommy as he managed to take on and beat players that were half his age and his skills looked almost as fresh as they had been twenty years ago when he played in the First Division with Blackpool.

Hutchison played his last League game for the club in March 1991 and at the end of that season was presented with a PFA Merit Award for his contribution to the game – 794 League appearances is a figure that will not be matched by too many people in the next 100 years! Hutchison left Swansea to become Football in the Community Officer for Merthyr Tydfil – passing on his experiences and knowledge from the game to others.

Leighton James
1980-1983

| League Appearances | 98 | League Goals | 27 |

Leighton James had already been recognised by his country at Schoolboy level before he signed for Burnley way back in 1968. It took the full Welsh selectors just three years to recognise that they had a talented winger in their midst and, in October 1971, he became one of the youngest people ever to be capped by Wales when he appeared against Czechoslovakia in Prague.

The following season he was instrumental in Burnley's Second Division Championship season, but by the end of the 1974/75 season he was on his way to the Baseball Ground after Don Mackay paid £310,000 to make him a Derby player. Two years passed at Derby, one of them as the club's top scorer before another move – this time to Loftus Road, a move that did not work out for James. Less than a year after moving to London he was back up north, returning to Burnley for £165,000 – a then-club-record transfer fee.

However, Burnley were soon relegated to the Third Division and James was on the move once again, this time back to Wales as John Toshack bought him for Swansea for the sum of £130,000 towards the end of the 1979/80 season. James was intended as one of the last pieces in the Swansea jigsaw as Toshack looked for promotion to the top flight, and he was soon repaying the faith that had been shown in him with his first hat-trick for the club on 11 October 1980 against his former club Derby County. Leighton added another triple to his collection when he achieved the same feat against Bolton at the Vetch on 28 February 1981 – two penalties and a twenty-five-yard screamer!

James was already the club's top scorer in that 1980/81 season when the side went into the final week knowing that promotion to the First Division was in their grasp. After Chelsea were dispatched 3-0 at the Vetch, James was on target in the 2-2 draw with Luton – a game that Swansea thoroughly deserved to win. So to Preston, and it was James who set the Swans' promotion wagon on course when he scored the first goal to take Swansea into the First Division for the first time in their history.

James was one of a posse of players who helped create records in the 1981/82 season when Wales named six internationals from Swansea in their side – a Welsh record to this day and one that is unlikely ever to be matched or beaten. James continued his goalscoring prowess during the course of that First Division season as well – including one of the goals as Manchester United were beaten 2-0 at the Vetch. However, as the tide began to turn at Swansea in the 1982/83 season, James was on his way out of the club and, after 27 League goals in two-and-a-half seasons he was on his way to Sunderland on a free transfer in January 1983. As it turned out, Swansea was the last club where James spent any notable time as he moved to Bury in 1984, Newport in 1985 and back to Burnley again in 1986. He made his last impact in League football in May 1987 when his goals kept Burnley in the League at the expense of Lincoln.

49

A coaching spell at Bradford and management jobs at Gainsborough Trinity, Morecambe and Llanelli Town followed and Leighton James can now be heard giving his views on sport in Wales on the weeknight sports phone-in on Real Radio as well as a contract with the BBC. A keen Swansea fan still, with a passion off the pitch that he certainly showed on it, Leighton wrote the foreword for Keith's 1999 edition of *Come on Cymru 2000!*

Robbie James
1973-1983, 1988-1990

| League Appearances | 478 | League Goals | 118 |

Harry Gregg saw Robbie James play at a very young age and knew straight away that he had unearthed a local talent at just the right age. After shining in both the Welsh League and the Football Combination, James was given his chance in the first team, along with Alan Curtis, in the last game of the 1972/73 season when Charlton Athletic visited the Vetch. James shone on that debut and, as the Swans signed off the season with a 2-1 victory, Gregg's faith looked to be paying early dividends.

A stocky midfielder, there was nothing more appetising to a Swans fan of the time than to see Robbie James pick up the ball in midfield and run at defenders. Particularly in the later stages of his career, defenders just seemed to bounce off him and, as a result, some very vital goals were scored by Robbie.

The team that was initially established by Harry Griffiths, and further led by John Toshack, was built around some very good local talent and James was no exception to that rule. As the club celebrated successive promotions in 1978 and 1979, James played no small part in the success that was gripping south-west Wales. During that two-year period, James found himself with a hat-trick to his name on three occasions, the first of which came in the 8-0 victory over Hartlepool – still the club's record League victory. Further hat-tricks against Newport County (League) and Kidderminster Harriers (Welsh Cup) and the Swans were back in the Second Division and rising fast.

Two years later James experienced his greatest day in a Swansea shirt when he celebrated promotion to the First Division with the Swans with a victory at Preston and, as they surprised most of the First Division the following season, it was the name of James who was making a real mark on the scoresheets. Ninety-nine League goals was his total when Swansea were relegated in 1983 and, as financial problems began to grip the club, he was sold to Stoke City for £160,000. However, he was unable to reproduce the form that he had at Swansea and further moves followed to QPR and Leicester City. Leicester decided that Robbie's waistline was not overly helpful to League football and released him in 1988, but the name was enough to persuade Swansea to bring Robbie back home and he was given the captain's armband to celebrate another promotion with the Swans, this time via the play-offs in 1988. Even when in confrontation with then-chairman Doug Sharp over moving expenses he still played and gave 100 per cent to the Swansea cause. A total of 16 further League goals in 90 appearances followed in that second spell for Swansea before he left the club again in the summer of 1990 to join Bradford in part of a settlement over the court action against Bradford in relation to Terry Yorath.

He again returned to south Wales and Stebonheath Park, Llanelli where he played League football for the local side but tragedy struck in 1996 when he collapsed and died during a League game – a sad and premature loss to the game of football.

Mike Johnson
1958-1966

| League Appearances | 165 | League Goals | 0 |

There was much criticism of the club in the summer of 1957 with the local press printing many letters from fans about the fact that there were no new signings coming into the club. Ron Burgess, though, was convinced that he had the players to challenge for promotion. Burgess did make some additions to the playing staff at the Vetch, signing Mike Johnson along with Barry Jones on amateur terms. Johnson plied his trade for two years before turning professional in the summer of 1959.

In his second season as a professional Johnson saw the club struggling near the foot of the Second Division. Indeed, towards the end of 1959 they found themselves at the bottom of the division and looking certainties for relegation. However, a few victories at the start of 1961 saw them moving up the table and a great escape act looked possible. During February 1961, the Swans were due to entertain runaway leaders Sheffield United at the Vetch. With Mel Nurse away on international duty, it fell to Johnson to stand in for him. The consensus was that the Swans would be beaten by the leaders but Johnson was outstanding and the team gained an unexpected two points.

By the time the following February had arrived, there were fresh rumours concerning Mel Nurse. The general consensus was that he was to leave the club. These rumours had surfaced before but had always been denied by the club. This time there was no denial, which just fuelled the speculation. With regular centre half Graham Williams suffering from a broken leg it was Johnson that was selected at centre half as his replacement. Because of this, manager Trevor Morris announced that the club had a 'wealth of centre half talent' and Nurse was allowed to leave.

As the 1963/64 season arrived, the Swans were struggling in the League and gates were down at the Vetch. However, it was not League form that captured the imagination of the fans that season but the FA Cup. It all started so innocently with a tie against Barrow in the third round. However, it was a very special day for Johnson as he captained the side for the first time in a 4-1 victory for the Swans. Further ties followed for the club against Sheffield United and Stoke before they were drawn against Liverpool in the quarter-finals. There was no doubt in the experts' minds that Liverpool were on their way to the next round. However, Johnson and his teammates had different ideas and the defence performed heroically in a famous 2-1 victory for the Swans. Johnson was said to have 'defended as if his life depended on it' at one stage as Liverpool looked for the equaliser. It never came and, despite a semi final defeat against Preston, Johnson had come so close to being the first Swansea captain to lead his side out at Wembley.

Mike Johnson played at the Vetch for two more seasons before leaving in 1966.

Cliff Jones
1952-1958

| League Appearances | 167 | League Goals | 48 |

There are several footballing dynasties who have appeared at the Vetch during the ninety-odd years of our history and Cliff Jones is part of one of the largest ones. Following on from the appearances of his father Ivor (Swansea, West Bromwich Albion and Wales), uncle Bryn (Wolverhampton Wanderers, Norwich, Arsenal and Wales) and his brother Brin (Swansea, Newport, Bournemouth, Northampton and Watford) Cliff was noticed while captaining Swansea Schoolboys in their 1-0 Schools' Shield final victory over Manchester.

He signed terms for Swansea in October 1952 and went on to play in over 160 games for the side, scoring 47 goals and winning his first Welsh cap at the age of nineteen. During the course of the 1956/57 season, he asked for a transfer away from the Vetch. The request was turned down but it was a temporary postponement. On the opening day of the 1957/58 season the Swans hammered Lincoln 5-1 but it was not a happy start for Jones, who missed a penalty in what was to be his last season in a Swansea shirt.

In March 1958 after several rumours surrounding Jones, the board issued a statement to say that they had acceded to his 'persistent demands for first-team football.' Within an eventful two weeks, which surrounded the Munich air disaster, Jones had signed for Tottenham. The fee involved, £35,000, was a new UK record. Ted Drake, who had missed out on Jones, declared that Spurs had 'the best winger in Britain.' That deal assisted Swansea in recording a record profit in the AGM at the end of that season.

He quickly established himself as a key player in the side that won four major trophies at the start of the 1960s, including the League and FA Cup double in 1961. He won a total of 59 Welsh caps in a career that, after another FA Cup triumph in 1967, ended at Craven Cottage and a spell with Fulham.

Ivor Jones
1920-1922

| League Appearances | 65 | League Goals | 14 |

Ivor Jones was the first of the Jones footballing dynasty to appear for the club. He was later succeeded by his two sons, Cliff and Brin, who made almost 300 appearances between them in the 1950s.

Ivor was signed by Swans manager Joe Bradshaw when he was just a teenager playing for Caerphilly. He had caught Bradshaw's eye when he appeared against the Swans' reserve side and he went on to captivate the Vetch Field crowds with his brilliance on the pitch. Indeed, within twelve months of arriving at the Vetch his performances earned him the first of 10 Welsh caps when he played against Ireland in 1920. This was a notable date in the history of the club as it made Jones the first player to be capped by his country while playing for the Swans. Such was his ability that he had played just 14 Southern League games when he made his international debut.

In 1922 the Swans created a first. Amid rumours that the English FA wanted to ban Welsh clubs from its premier competition, Jones scored the only goal that took the Swans into the third round of the competition for the first time. It was not a successful venture, as they were beaten 4-0 by Millwall at the Vetch, but it was a step forward as far as the club was concerned.

He had played just 66 League games for the club when he was surprisingly sold to West Bromwich Albion for a then-club-record fee of £2,500. This sparked fury among the Swansea crowd who were not best pleased that their favourite had been sold. For the day the transfer fee was a huge sum that was reflective of Jones' talents but that did not make the sale any less painful. The fans voted with their feet and for the first game after the sale just 3,000 people turned up to see Bristol Rovers on 15 April 1922. The Swans, though, showed little signs of missing Jones as they scored eight goals.

Ivor Jones may have only played on the Vetch staff for two years but he had made an impression and few who had seen him play forgot the style in which he did so.

Rory Keane
1947-1954

League Appearances 164 **League Goals** 0

As the name suggests, Rory Keane was born and bred in Ireland. Indeed, it was with Limerick that Swansea first saw him in action and the club brought him over the Irish Sea during the summer of 1947 to plug a gap that they felt they had at full-back.

Certainly part of Swansea's success at the end of the 1940s can be put down to the performances of Keane and it was no surprise to Swansea fans of the time when he was called up for his first international appearance for the Republic of Ireland against Switzerland in 1949 – the first of 4 caps that he was awarded during that year. But, even more strangely that season, Keane was also capped by Northern Ireland when he played against Scotland – one of only a few players that have managed the feat of playing for both Irelands at international level. Keane was also instrumental in the Swans' progress to the fourth round of

53

the FA Cup during this season. The game brought back memories of a famous victory over the same side in the same competition almost twenty-five years previously. With the Swans already one down it was Keane who gave away the penalty for the second goal. A Lewis header was going into the goal when Keane rose like a goalkeeper to punch the ball over the bar. A certain sending off these days, Keane just had to suffer as Arsenal tucked away the resulting penalty to put the London side two up.

The 1949/50 season was to be the highlight of Keane's career. However, he broke his leg towards the end of the season and the record books show that he never ever recovered to be the same sort of player after that. However, he managed to stay at the Vetch for a further six seasons past that, making a total of 164 League appearances for the club, although he failed to find the net in any of those games.

Keane died early in 2004.

Tom Kiley
1947-1957

League Appearances   129   League Goals   2

Tom Kiley had been a member of the Swansea Schoolboys' side before he joined Arsenal, and had made 3 appearances for the Welsh international Schoolboys' team before he joined the Royal Air Force. As the Second World War ended he appeared in the Welsh League side and, on leaving the Air Force in 1947, he joined the Swans.

His early years at the Vetch were spent in the Welsh League or combination football and his performances there eventually led to him making his first-team debut in a goalless draw at Queens Park Rangers in 1950. Kiley's early years at the Vetch were blighted by injury, the worst of which came in February 1953 when he fractured his leg. Kiley fought back from this injury and, during the course of the 1954/55 season, he was selected as a reserve for the full Welsh side. A further knock followed in November 1956 when he suffered a serious knee injury during training and he ended up having to undergo an operation in hospital. It was four months before Kiley was able to return to first-team action but by that time the damage had been done and, after just a handful more games, he was forced to retire from football. It is part of Swansea soccer folklore that had it not been for the untimely injuries to Kiley the Swans would have been promoted to the First Division, and it was only the sides of this period and that of 1980/81 that were ever good enough to achieve that feat.

Kiley had been known as the 'master of the middle' during his time with Swansea and the record books show some sterling performances from the home-grown lad during the early seasons after the Second World War ended. The statistics show that Kiley was one of the unluckiest players that Swansea ever had as far as injuries were concerned. Kiley, though, took a keen interest in the Swans after retiring from the game and as Harry Griffiths took the side close to promotion in 1976/77, Kiley wrote to the *South Wales Evening Post* to congratulate Griffiths on his work. He also urged the supporters to get behind the players to lift them to promotion.

John King
1950-1964

| League Appearances | 363 | League Goals | 0 |

John King held the record number of appearances for the club as a goalkeeper until Roger Freestone broke the record late in the 1990s. In total he played for the club in 368 League games over a fourteen-year period between 1950 and 1964. However, his debut was not one that he would remember for too long as he picked the ball out of the back of his goal five times as the Swans went down 5-0 at Birmingham City. King was just a seventeen-year-old amateur at that time and he went on from that to complete his national service. However, once that was up he was back in the side and, in 1955, his performances earned him his one and only Welsh cap when he was part of a victorious Welsh side that triumphed 2-1 over England at Ninian Park.

Ten years had passed when Swansea brought Noel Dwyer to the club in 1960 but King kept his place initially before the goalkeeping duties started to be shared out between King and Dwyer. The club awarded King a benefit of £1,000 in February 1961, shortly after he had helped Swansea to a fourth round FA Cup win over Preston North End.

King decided that it was time to call it a day at the end of the 1963/64 season and he emigrated to Australia where he died in 1982, aged just forty-nine.

Bob Latchford
1981-1984

| League Appearances | 87 | League Goals | 35 |

Bob Latchford was capped by England while at Everton and, as the Swans prepared for their first season in the top flight, his pedigree persuaded John Toshack to part with £125,000 of the club's money to bring Latchford to the Vetch.

Few who saw Latchford's League debut for the club will forget it as well. It was a bright sunny day at the Vetch on 29 August 1981 with the opponents being Leeds United. The Swans were soon one up through Charles but at the interval settled for a 1-1 scoreline after Parlane equalised for the visitors. As the second half started it turned into the Latchford show. Just forty-five seconds after the restart he had notched his first goal in a Swansea shirt to put the club back ahead. That, though, was just the start and ten minutes later the scoreline read Swansea City 4 Leeds United 1 – Latchford had achieved the honour of scoring the Swans' first hat-trick in the top flight in an incredible spell of football.

Latchford found himself back on target in the next game – a 2-1 win at Brighton – and all of a sudden Swansea were top of the Football League and Latchford was already a folk hero in south west Wales. Of course, two games in League tables show nothing but by the time Latchford had scored the winning goal at Stoke in October, Swansea were on top of the League again and people were beginning to stand up and notice that this team meant business. Latchford finished the season with 12 goals from 31 League appearances, the Swans finished sixth and everything was looking rosy at the Vetch for a Championship challenge the following season. Latchford himself was now again on the verge of the England squad. Three games into the 1982/83 season there was no reason to suspect that those thoughts would have been anything but true. Three games – two wins and a draw – four goals from Latchford, including a hat-trick against Norwich at the Vetch, and everything seemed like a case of déjà vu. That, though, was as good as that season got. Latchford found himself on the scoresheet more often (15 goals) but Swansea could not get the results that they so desperately needed and, after two seasons, they were back on their way into the Second Division.

Bob had made his impression on Swansea and with 27 goals in the League during those two seasons he remains Swansea's highest League goalscorer in the top flight, and it's a safe bet that he will hold that record for quite some time! The side that had been so successful in the top flight began to break up. Latchford was no exception and he moved on from Swansea, but not without the thanks of the fans who so often had celebrated a goal from Big Bob.

Sid Lawrence
1930-1939

League Appearances 312 **League Goals** 9

Sid Lawrence was signed for the Swans having worked his way through the ranks at the club. He made his first-team debut halfway through the 1930/31 season. It did not take long for young full-back Sid to establish himself in the Swans' defence, but it also sparked several rumours of a possible transfer to a bigger club.

However, it was not just the top clubs that were watching. In 1932/33 he won the first of his 8 Welsh caps when he lined up against Northern Ireland. Despite a good debut for his country, he kept his feet firmly on the ground and was a popular player both with his teammates and the supporters.

Lawrence made his final appearance for Wales against Scotland in 1936. However, as the spring of 1939 arrived, several Swans players were placed on the 'open to transfer' list – Lawrence being one of them. As the squad looked likely to be decimated it wasn't helped by the resignation of manager Neil Harris, who moved to Swindon in the June. It didn't take long for him to raid his old club and Lawrence, along with Bill Irvine, joined Harris at the County Ground where he finished his career.

Andrew Legg
1988-1993

| League Appearances | 157 | League Goals | 29 |

Andrew Legg had just turned twenty-two when he was signed for the Swans by then-manager Terry Yorath. Legg had been putting in some impressive performances for his non-league side Briton Ferry when he moved to the Swans.

The side had just won promotion to the Third Division via the play-offs and Yorath felt that Legg could offer his side something as he prepared for life in the higher division. As managers came and went, Legg remained an important part of the Swansea side for five years. Indeed, Legg tormented the Liverpool defence during a 0-0 draw in the FA Cup in 1990 and scored a goal at Stoke a couple of years later that the Swans fans will still talk about today. It was here that he developed his long throw-in.

Legg's impressive form for the Swans soon drew the attention of other clubs and it was in 1993 that Frank Burrows accepted an offer of £275,000 from Notts County, and Legg was on his way. He had played a total of 207 games for the Swans and found the net on 38 occasions when he left. Two-and-a-half seasons followed for Legg at Meadow Lane where he made a further 123 appearances before Birmingham City expressed an interest and a £250,000 move to St Andrews followed. He was an instant hit at the Midlands side and soon settled down on the left wing. At one stage, Legg held the world record for a throw-in of 44.54m, which was eventually beaten in 1997.

His form for Birmingham earned him international recognition and to date he has won 6 full caps for Wales. However, at the end of the 1997/98 season he found himself unable to agree new terms with Birmingham and, after a brief spell with Ipswich on loan, he was on the move again – this time to Reading, who he joined for £75,000. Legg found himself unable to settle at Reading and a further loan spell came at Peterborough before he moved to Cardiff City on a free transfer in 1998. Legg won three promotions with Cardiff and was part of the Cardiff squad that triumphed in the play off final in 2003. He will say that his career has flourished at Ninian Park and the fans have taken to 'Andy the Jack'. They even voted him Player of the Season on two occasions; proof if any that bridges can be built between the clubs.

57

In his career Legg made over 600 appearances for his various clubs as well as finding the net on over 50 occasions. Sadly, he was forced to retire from his post as player-coach at Peterborough, who he joined after Cardiff, when he was diagnosed with cancer. Legg is treating that battle with the same will and determination that he showed during his playing career and it is a battle that we all hope he wins.

Dudley Lewis
1979-1989

League Appearances   232   League Goals   2

Dudley Lewis was already a Welsh Schoolboy international when he signed apprentice forms at the Vetch in the late 1970s before signing his first professional contract just six months later. John Toshack, who at the time was in the process of leading his side into the top flight for the first time, was always one to take a managerial gamble and he saw potential in Lewis, so much so that he handed him his debut in 1980/81 against fellow promotion chasers Notts County. Lewis was just a teenager who captained the youth team, but performed well despite the Swans going down to a 2-1 defeat. Toshack liked what he saw and, despite leaving him out for the next game, brought him back for a game against Bolton at the Vetch. Lewis was outstanding as sweeper as the Swans won 3-0 and the promotion wagon was back on track.

On the last day of that season against Preston, Lewis put in another impressive display and, as the final whistle blew to signal the Swans' promotion, it was Lewis that Toshack searched out as the players hugged each other – fully appreciative of the job that the eighteen-year-old had done for him.

Lewis did not manage to hold down a regular place during the first season in the top flight but by the time the Swans were relegated at the end of the 1982/83 season he was a regular. As the Swans slid back down the Football League, Lewis was constantly putting in quality performances at the heart of defence but only won 1 Welsh cap, a substitute appearance against Brazil in Cardiff – a game Wales drew 1-1.

In nine seasons at the Vetch Dudley appeared in 230 League games for the club. A broken leg in a FA Cup fourth round tie against Hull at the Vetch signalled the start of the end of his time at the Vetch and in the summer of 1989 – twelve months after helping the Swans to promotion – he was on his way to Huddersfield. He never settled as a Terrier and, after a loan spell with Halifax Town, he moved to Wrexham where he called a halt to his career at the end of the 1991/92 season.

Wilf Lewis
1926-1928

| League Appearances | 65 | League Goals | 43 |

Wilf Lewis signed professional terms for the Swans back in 1925 but struggled in the early days to establish himself as a regular in the first team. He had only made a handful of appearances for the club when, on 27 December 1926, he netted a hat-trick for the club in a 3-0 win over Oldham Athletic at the Vetch. That was enough to persuade the Welsh selectors that he had a talent for international football and shortly afterwards he made his debut for his country in a 3-3 draw with England.

The 1927/28 season, however, was the making of Lewis and he netted in total 25 goals in 39 League games. The highlight of those goals was his second hat-trick in a 6-3 victory over South Shields – a result made the more remarkable by the fact that until the last quarter of an hour Swansea were always behind. The Swans finished sixth in the division that season – with Wilf responsible for one-third of their total goals scored!

The following season, Lewis continued his goal-scoring exploits and it was not a surprise when, in November 1928, he was on his way to Huddersfield Town. The fee involved in the transfer was £6,500 – a then-record transfer fee in for the club. The move, however, shocked the fans, who had seen Lewis as the natural successor to Jack Fowler – who managed just one more goal before he too was on his way out of the Vetch. After his short spell at Huddersfield he left to join Derby County, where he only made 8 appearances. Strangely, those appearances generated 3 goals although it was not enough for Derby to take a chance on him and he was released. He moved to non-league football to play for Yeovil Town.

Despite his limited number of appearances for his three League clubs Lewis still managed to get himself capped 6 times by Wales and had one of the most prolific goal-scoring records in the club's history.

Billy Lucas
1948-1954, Manager 1967-1969

| League Appearances | 205 | League Goals | 35 |

Billy Lucas was part of the Swansea Championship-winning side of 1948/49 and, when he arrived at the Vetch prior to the start of that season, he was described as the missing link that would mean the Swans could build on the relative success of the previous season.

It was at Swindon that Lucas started his career prior to the outbreak of the Second World War and during that six-year period he was part of the Wales team that competed in victory internationals. When the war finished he returned to the County Ground and Swindon Town. It took £11,000 for manager Billy McCandless to prise him away from Swindon – a figure that was a then-club record. It was money well spent and Lucas was highly instrumental in arguably Swansea's best ever season as they topped the League with sixty-two points on the board. His displays did not go unnoticed at international level either and he gained the first of 7 Welsh caps in October

1949 when he played against Scotland at Ninian Park. Four more years followed at the Vetch before he departed for Newport County and management in 1953, leaving a hole that Swansea struggled to fill. Eight years followed for Billy in the Newport hot seat, although many of those were spent battling the financial disadvantages at Somerton Park. Within twelve months, though, Lucas was back in the manager's chair for a second spell and lasted a further six years in charge before returning to Swansea to take charge in 1967.

Unfortunately for Lucas his return to the Vetch saw the side struggling to remain in the Third Division and he was unable to save them from relegation. Another season-and-a-half followed but Lucas was unable to take the Swans back up and he returned again to Newport in 1969 for another six-year spell – twenty years in total being his time in the manager's seat at Newport.

Upon leaving the club again in 1975 Lucas retired from football completely to concentrate on his business, leaving behind a career that had lasted close on forty years.

John Mahoney
1979-1983

League Appearances   110   League Goals   0

John Mahoney was born and bred in Cardiff and learned to play football in the back streets of the city with his cousin, Swansea's finest manager, John Toshack. Mahoney, though, was to leave Cardiff when his father, a rugby player, moved north to become a rugby league professional. He never followed his father into rugby and continued to ply his trade with a round ball. He played local football for Ashton United when he was spotted by the scouts of Crewe Alexandra, where he fully began his career.

Crewe was not a long stopover for Mahoney as they struggled to develop his career and Stoke City took John on and turned him into a quality midfielder. In 1972 he was part of the Stoke side that won the League Cup and, after scoring 25 goals, he was on the move to Ayresome Park and a spell with Middlesbrough. When Toshack went into management at Swansea he persuaded his cousin to link up with him and Mahoney was part of the successful Swansea side of the late 1970s and the early 1980s. He made his Swansea debut in a League Cup victory over Bournemouth and established himself very quickly in the Swansea side.

The Swans were on the move and Mahoney was going with them as they celebrated three promotions in four seasons to end in the First Division. He played his part in those glory years and felt it as much as anyone as the club looked favourites for relegation in the 1982/83 season. Sadly for Mahoney he never experienced the end of that season as he broke his leg in a game against Brighton in March 1983, which ended his playing career.

Swansea rewarded his loyalty with a position on the backroom staff, but he missed the day-to-day football side of things and he moved into management himself at Bangor City. From Bangor he moved to Newport County where he was manager when the club went out of existence, and he returned to Bangor to take control of the club again.

Chris Marustik
1978-1985

| League Appearances | 152 | League Goals | 11 |

Chris Marustik was the son of a Czech immigrant and caught the eye of Swans manager Harry Griffiths when he was in action for Swansea Schoolboys. He signed apprentice terms at the Vetch under Griffiths. Marustik played in a pre-season friendly against Everton that raised money for Harry Griffiths' widow as a token of appreciation for his services. Chris was still two weeks short of his sixteenth birthday at that time but his performance caught the eye of the supporters. Two weeks later, as he turned sixteen, he signed his first professional contract for the club.

He made his debut for the club in August 1978 when the Swans upset the form book and held the mighty Tottenham Hotspur to a 2-2 draw at the Vetch. His League debut came in May 1979 when the Swans were beaten 2-0 at Peterborough United. With the Swans completing promotion that season, two seasons were to follow in the Second Division. The first of those seasons saw Marustik play 10 games. A similar figure followed the next season but, as the Swans embarked on a first campaign in the First Division he found himself out of the side initially – he was back in at the end of the season. However, it was not just the Swans' first team that he found himself in, but also the Wales squad. While some of his teammates were taking the press plaudits and the cheers of the supporters, Marustik was one of the unsung heroes of the period and the Welsh cap was recognition of his efforts and displays when in the team.

He had been nurtured and developed by a combination of John Toshack, John Mahoney and Les Chappell since he was discovered by Griffiths. However, the Swansea dream was turning sour and relegations in 1983 and 1984 were hitting hard as financial problems began to cripple the club. In October 1985, two months before a winding-up order, Marustik left the Swans to join near-neighbours Cardiff City. However, he found his way hampered by injury at Ninian Park and in two seasons he managed just 43 League appearances before he left League football to play for Barry Town. Chris still lives and works in Swansea.

Billy McCandless
Manager 1947-1955

Debate rages long and hard about the various assets of football managers during their time but very few will query the inclusion in this book of Billy McCandless when mentioning the period covering the 1930s and 1940s.

A quick glance at the McCandless CV will reveal that he holds the unique record of taking Newport County, Cardiff City and Swansea City to the Third Division (South) Championship. However, it was not only off the pitch that McCandless made his name. As a player with Linfield he played in three Irish Cup finals before moving to Scotland and a spell with Glasgow Rangers which saw him gain seven League Championship medals. Billy made his move into management in 1930, taking charge at Ballymena United before moving on to Dundee and then, in 1937, Newport County. It was at Somerton Park that he picked up his first Championship in 1938/39 before moving on to Cardiff City in 1946. In his first season in the hot seat there the Bluebirds picked up the second title for McCandless, finishing the season seven points clear at the top of the League.

While it was all success at Cardiff, at that time Swansea were struggling. But when Billy arrived at the Vetch in 1947 they were on a recovery, having only been beaten once in their previous ten games. But the effect that he had was almost instant and, in that first season, the Swans finished fifth, which gave great optimism for the season ahead. Fans through the gates backed this optimism and it was arguably the 1948/49 season that saw Swansea play some of their best ever football. During the 1948/49 campaign Billy led the Swans to twenty-seven victories, including seventeen in succession at home and a then-record sixty-two points in a season. It was an exciting time at the Vetch, as the Swans managed a positive goal difference of 53, the best ever registered by a Swansea side. The Championship was won by the same margin as Billy managed at Cardiff – seven points – and the Swans were back in the Second Division.

The following season was another good one for Billy as he led his new troops to finish two places above the team he had left behind for Swansea and there was no doubt that Billy's talents on and off the pitch were reflected in his overall success in the game.

Sadly, Billy died in 1955 but left behind a legacy at Swansea that included the Allchurch brothers and Mel Charles. There is little doubt that Billy McCandless holds the distinction of being one of Swansea's finest ever managers.

Sean McCarthy
1985-1988

League Appearances   91   League Goals   25

Sean McCarthy was a local player who was playing for Bridgend Town when he signed professional forms for the Swans in October 1985. For McCarthy, it was the realisation of a childhood dream in that he was playing for the side he supported, and he was determined to make the most of his opportunity.

In November 1985 he was selected for the first time in a Third Division game against Chesterfield – a game that ended in a 1-1 draw. A month later, McCarthy was left wondering, along with his teammates of that time, if he still had an employer as the club went so close to extinction. The club, as we know, was saved and McCarthy established himself in the first team despite relegation from the Third Division that season.

A tough, no-nonsense centre forward, McCarthy was a player who frustrated the fans as often as he delighted them but in 1987/88 he did help the Swans to promotion with some vital goals, none more so than in the play-offs against Rotherham United and Torquay United. However, that game at Plainmoor was to provide the swansong for Sean as he moved to Plymouth Argyle in that close season for the sum of £50,000. He had played in a total of 113 games for the Swans and found the net on 38 occasions when he left.

Two seasons followed at Plymouth with 26 goals in 81 appearances before he made a £250,000 move to Valley Parade and Bradford City. He was an immediate success and in his three seasons there he ended each one as the club's top scorer as well as winning 'B' international honours for Wales. He was averaging one goal every other game when Oldham Athletic parted with £500,000 to take McCarthy to Boundary Park. A series of injuries blighted his early career at Oldham and a short loan spell at Bristol City followed. He returned to Oldham where he scored a further 48 goals in 165 appearances before making the move back down south to rejoin Plymouth. After three more years at Home Park he made the short trip up the A38 to Exeter where he was registered as a player until 2002

In total, during his career Sean has made over 640 appearances and at the time of writing has 220 goals to his credit, including 174 in the League.

Jimmy McLaughlin
1963-1967, 1972-1974

| League Appearances | 151 | League Goals | 46 |

Jimmy McLaughlin had a brief spell at Birmingham City before signing for Shrewsbury Town in the summer of 1960, winning his first cap for his country (Northern Ireland) when he was at Gay Meadow. One hundred goals in 340 appearances followed for the Shrews before Swansea manager Trevor Morris paid £16,000 to secure his services at the end of the 1962/63 season. The fee was a new record for the club at that stage, although the signing failed to capture the imagination with season ticket sales quite low.

McLaughlin was thrown in at the start of the following season for Swansea and he made an immediate impact as Swansea went on a run that would take them into the semi-finals of the FA Cup. His goals were against Stoke (fifth round), Liverpool (quarter-finals) and in the semi-final against Preston, which the Swans went on to lose 2-1 in the second half.

The following season McLaughlin notched his only Swansea hat-trick in a 5-0 win over Bournemouth, but two years later he was on the move again to join Peterborough in their new challenge of League football. It was a move that never worked out and just 8 appearances later he was back at Gay Meadow for a second spell with Shrewsbury, before retracing his steps back to Swansea with an appointment as player-coach. McLaughlin was later named as an assistant to Harry Gregg, along with Harry Griffiths.

In total he played just over 150 games for the Swans, finding the net on 47 occasions.

Lachlan McPherson
1924-1929

| League Appearances | 199 | League Goals | 28 |

Lachlan McPherson made an immediate impact at Swansea after joining the club from Notts County in 1924. He was part of the side that won the Third Division (South) Championship in 1924/25, finishing one point ahead of runners-up Plymouth Argyle. He had signed the previous summer with a reputation as a 'ball artist', equally at home at either wing half or inside forward. He had first been noticed by the Swansea manager Bradshaw on a pre-season tour of Denmark when he was playing for Notts County.

He made his debut at the start of the 1924/25 season in a 2-0 win over Swindon at the Vetch where, despite Jack Fowler grabbing both the goals, it was McPherson who caught the eye. However, it was not too long before the local press got critical of McPherson, claiming that he 'over-elaborated'.

McPherson, though, had long since shaken that criticism and during Swansea's run to the semi-finals of the FA Cup in 1925/26 he was instrumental in their success. Against Millwall he laid the foundations for the only goal of the game with just three minutes left in the tie. So, on 6 March, McPherson lined up against Arsenal and was given the task of man-marking the great Charlie Buchan. Not content with doing a superb job on this front, McPherson was also part of the move that put the Swans 1-0 up just before half-time. After winning that game 2-1, the FA Cup dream died when the Swans were beaten 3-0 by Bolton in the semi-finals.

At the start of the 1927/28 season, McPherson was given a more adventurous role within the team and responded by achieving the feat of successive hat-tricks in home matches. He netted three as Manchester City were beaten 5-3 and the second treble came in a 6-0 win over Wolverhampton Wanderers. The latter game also marked a piece of history for the Swans when the old 'double decker' stand at the west end of the ground was used for the first time. This was the first stand of its type to be built in Wales and was capable of seating 2,120 people.

Not surprisingly, this kind of form soon brought interest from the higher-up clubs and strong rumours were circulating the Vetch that he was on his way to Huddersfield Town. However, McPherson was not on his way just yet and spent another year at Swansea. After taking his total to 199 League games and 30 goals he left the club along with Ben Williams and joined Everton. His first return to the Vetch Field showed the fans what they had lost when he was inspirational as the Toffeemen ran out 5-2 victors. It was one of just 31 games that he played for Everton before leaving to join New Brighton in August 1932, where he ended his career.

Terry Medwin
1948-1956, Assistant Manager 1979-1983

| League Appearances | 147 | League Goals | 57 |

Terry Medwin had an early taste of life around the Vetch Field when he spent a large amount of time in his father's employment next door at Swansea Prison. However, it was not just the fact that he was growing up around the Vetch that bought him into the club – he was a talented footballer and Welsh Schoolboy honours followed for Medwin. He chose to sign for Swansea over a handful of higher-placed clubs in 1949.

However, Medwin had to be content with a reserve-team place for three years before his big chance came in a League match with Doncaster Rovers in 1952. What a dream debut he was to have, as he notched a goal within a minute of the game starting! Although the Swans were eventually to go and lose the game, however, the goal was enough to keep him his place in the side. Plenty of goals were to follow for the Swans – enough for him to be noticed by those in Cardiff. A first Welsh cap followed in 1953 against Northern Ireland and it was clear that Medwin was destined for bigger things than Swansea could maybe offer him.

Indeed, after the 1955/56 season Medwin was sold to Tottenham Hotspur for £18,000, where he made an immediate impact, scoring twice on his debut against Preston North End. That was enough to convince Spurs that he was designed to be in the side and four years as a regular followed. The 1960/61 season was legendary with Tottenham fans, as they won the League and FA Cup double, but Medwin was one of the unlucky players in the squad at that time, making only 15 appearances during the course of that historic season. The following season, though, he did gain some consolation with his place secured back in the side as Tottenham retained the FA Cup.

Sadly, Medwin was to see his career cut short in 1963 when he broke a leg during a tour to South Africa. Despite a couple of aborted comebacks Medwin was forced to admit defeat and, after a spell away from the game, he came back to coaching spells at Cardiff, Fulham and Norwich before being tempted back to Swansea as assistant manager to John Toshack. It was during that spell that Medwin was fortunate enough to be part of a revolution as Swansea climbed from the Fourth to the First Division in record time.

Ill health forced Medwin to retire completely from the game in 1983.

Andrew Melville
1985-1990

| League Appearances | 175 | League Goals | 23 |

Andrew Melville was born in Swansea and signed for his home-town side as soon as he was able to. He progressed through the ranks of the football club from a youth trainee and finally made his debut for the first team in a 3-1 home defeat by Bristol City in November 1985. Melville feared that he would be out of a job just a month later when the club folded due to its crippling debts but an eleventh-hour package saved the club and Melville found himself still playing for the side as 1986 dawned.

Melville was tried in a variety of positions at the start of his career but it was quickly established that a place in the centre of defence would be his best position. He was switched during the late 1980s to a spell up front that brought immediate dividends, but he was soon moved back to defence. Melville was a first-team regular by the time the Swans won promotion in 1988, the first side to be promoted from the Fourth Division via the play-offs. After a resounding finish to the season, Melville helped the team to a two-legged victory over Rotherham in the semi-finals and a nail-biting two-legged final victory over Torquay. By this time he was club captain, a position he was appointed to at the age of twenty, but his performances were drawing the attention of clubs in a higher position than Swansea and in 1990 they agreed to let him go to Oxford for the sum of £275,000 plus a percentage of any future transfer fee.

Melville found himself an instant success at Oxford and was virtually ever-present in the side for three seasons before joining Sunderland for a free transfer in the summer of 1993. It was not a great start at Roker Park for Melville as the side crashed 5-0 to Derby County on the opening day of the 1993/94 season and his first three seasons at Sunderland were spent at the bottom end of Division One.

When Peter Reid took over at the end of the 1994/95 season he was given a mission to keep the Wearsiders in the division; a feat that he managed. The following season saw Melville play 40 games as Sunderland completed a remarkable turnaround and won the Division One Championship. Melville was in the top flight and he acquitted himself well despite Sunderland's immediate relegation. He missed the last seven games due to a broken nose.

After a loan spell at Bradford City in 1998, Melville was back at Sunderland for the 1998/99 season and for the second time helped them to the title and a place in the Premiership. It was his last act with the club as he moved to Fulham during the close season on a free transfer. Melville made over 200 appearances for Fulham, serving under former teammate Chris Coleman before he moved to West Ham where he will seemingly end his career after retiring from international football towards the end of 2004, after the tenure of then-manager Mark Hughes ended. Melville won more then 50 caps for his country.

Tony Millington
1969-1974

League Appearances 178 **League Goals** 0

If you go back thirty years or so you will find a list of goalkeepers that have become favourites at the Vetch Field. Tony Millington is a member of that club.

After starting his career with West Bromwich Albion he moved to Crystal Palace in October 1964 before a further move to Peterborough followed in 1966. It was with Peterborough that he really established himself as a quality goalkeeper and, even to this day, he holds the record as the most-capped player while playing for the London Road outfit. He was brought to the Vetch at the start of the 1969/70 season, a season that was to see the Swans win promotion from the Fourth Division. During that campaign he kept a total of twenty clean sheets and much of the success of that season was credited to this factor.

He went on to stay at the Vetch for a period of five seasons, adding 8 caps to his Welsh tally during that period. He equalled a club record during the 1971/72 season when he kept five successive clean sheets – a record that was eventually beaten by both Dai Davies and Roger Freestone.

Millington played a total of 178 games for the Swans in the League and left the club at the end of the 1973/74 season.

Wilf Milne
1920-1937

| League Appearances | 586 | League Goals | 7 |

Wilf Milne, at the time of writing, still holds the record for the greatest number of appearances in a Swansea shirt, having appeared 657 times in his seventeen-year association with the club. Milne stood at just 5ft 8in and weighed in at under 12 stone, but was classed as a giant in many respects.

In August 1920, Swansea played their first ever game in the Football League and Milne was on the team sheet as Swansea lost 3-0 at Portsmouth. Milne was known in the game for his tackling ability and not for his goalscoring prowess. In fact, he appeared in 585 League games for the Swans but only found himself on the scoresheet twice, both from the penalty spot. Indeed, it was 501 League games into his Swansea career before he netted for the first time, and the only other goal he scored came at the end of the 1933/34 season when he scored a goal that saved Swansea from relegation.

Wilf was a part of Swansea's Championship-winning squad of 1924/25 and played a major part in their march to the FA Cup semi-finals in 1926. Milne also played in goal for two matches at the end of his Swansea career. They were the last two matches of his career with the club as well. On the way to two games in three days in the Midlands stiffness developed in the goalkeeper Moore's knees. This stiffness meant that he was ruled out of both matches and Milne was the only available substitute. Milne, as ever, did not let the club down and was congratulated by all for a superb display in a 0-0 draw. However, the fairytale finish ended there as he took his place in goal for the next game, his last for the club. Picking the ball out of the back of the net six times is not how Milne would have visualised his career ending, but it took nothing away from the service that he had shown the club.

At the end of the 1936/37 season the club arranged a special benefit match for Milne. Milne was the last of the promotion side of thirteen years earlier to part with the club. As if to mark the occasion with suitable imagery, at the same time the Swansea authorities were taking up tramlines. It was indeed the end of an era in more ways than one.

Jan Molby
1996-1997

| League Appearances | 41 | League Goals | 8 |

It seems hard to believe that Jan Molby was only at Swansea City for eighteen months when you consider all that happened at the Vetch during that time. Already a Danish international, Jan joined Liverpool from Ajax in the summer of 1984 for a fee of £575,000. A dominant midfield figure, he was designed to replace Graham Souness in the Liverpool midfield and in only his second season for the club he helped them to the then-rare feat of League and FA Cup double. Molby was distraught in April 1989 when he was in the Liverpool side that played in the fateful

FA Cup semi-final at Hillsborough and, although Liverpool eventually won the FA Cup that season, Molby's pain that day in Sheffield was evident for all to see.

A further League Championship followed the next season but Molby's appearances in a Liverpool shirt were starting to be restricted by injury. Brief loan spells at Barnsley and Norwich followed and Molby left Liverpool with 61 goals in 292 games to his credit.

It was under the most bizarre circumstances that Molby found himself at Swansea. Owner Doug Sharpe was trying to sell the club and Midlands businessman Michael Thompson was on the verge of taking over. Thompson was promising a big-name manager and the name of Molby had been linked, along with his former Liverpool colleague Ian Rush. Thompson, though, had a different version of a big name to Swansea fans and the unknown Kevin Cullis was appointed from non-league side Cradley Heath. He was soon found to be completely out of his depth. Molby was present at the Vetch when Cullis made his managerial bow for the club against Swindon – a game that the Swans lost 1-0. Molby was under discussion with the club to join as a player but whether he could have foreseen the events of the next seven days we will never know.

Swansea lost a League game 4-0 at Blackpool but Cullis was nowhere to be seen. The reason was that Doug Sharpe had cornered Thompson at a service station on the M6 and basically taken the club back, meaning that effectively both were out of employment. If nothing else Sharpe proved his Swansea credentials that night. Swansea were looking favourites for relegation and Molby was given his first managerial opportunity with just under three months to save the club. While he failed in that task, performances improved dramatically towards the end of the season and Molby looked forward to a successful season in charge ahead.

Molby almost emulated the achievements of another Liverpool legend, John Toshack, nearly twenty years earlier. After a sluggish start to the season, Molby turned the Swans around and led them out at Wembley in May 1997 for the play-off final. By far the form team, and also the better team on the day, Swansea were agonisingly beaten in the last minute by a twice-taken John Frain free-kick for the opposition. Molby watched in devastation as his players dropped to the floor but picked them up to show their appreciation of the support.

Swansea changed owners again in the close season and new owners Silver Shield never took to Molby. He was sacked in October 1997. Two spells in management followed – Kidderminster, who he took into the Football League, and Hull, but neither worked out for the big Danish man. After leaving Hull, Molby returned to Kidderminster for a second spell but was sacked early in the 2004/05 season. He is now a pundit for BBC Radio Manchester.

Trevor Morris
Manager 1958-1965

Trevor Morris was a player who saw his career end very prematurely in 1941 when he suffered a broken leg in a game between Cardiff City and Bristol City during the December of that year. It was that side that gave him his return to football when they offered him the post of assistant secretary in 1946, being promoted to secretary-manager when Cyril Spiers resigned the post. However, in 1958 he moved to Swansea Town as general manager – a move that was to last for seven years.

Although Swansea were hardly setting the world alight during this period, Morris was in charge of the side that entered the 1963/64 season looking for another year of Second Division survival. However, Morris took the side on a run that is still talked about today. As the draw for the third round of the FA Cup was made, Swansea against Barrow was not exactly one of the ties of the round. But Swansea were victorious by four goals to one and a fourth round trip to Bramall Lane beckoned. Despite being the underdogs, Swansea gained a draw and triumphed 4-0 in the replay at the Vetch to advance into the fifth round and a date at Stoke. Again a replay was needed but goals from McLaughlin and Todd led Swansea into the quarter-finals and a famous date with Liverpool. Early goals from McLaughlin and Eddie Thomas put the Swans up by two goals but one pulled back led to many nervous moments before holding out, and a semi-final encounter with Preston was on the agenda. Swansea were looking to emulate Cardiff City by reaching the final of the competition and after forty-five minutes they found themselves a goal up through McLaughlin, but it was not to be as Preston hit back with two goals to reach the final themselves.

That was to be the high point of Morris's Swansea career as the side were relegated back to the Third Division the following season and he resigned. A brief spell at Somerton Park followed before Morris took up a position as secretary of the Welsh FA.

Morris died at his home in February 2003.

Dai Nicholas
1924-1930

| League Appearances | 151 | League Goals | 14 |

Dai Nicholas had two spells at Swansea during an eventful career in football. He was an amateur for the club in the years leading up to the First World War but left the club to play for Merthyr Town. However, as the war ended Nicholas found himself on the move again as he joined Stoke, and it was there that he earned his first cap for Wales when he played against Scotland in 1923. During the course of the 1924/25 Championship season Swansea brought Nicholas 'back home', and he made his debut for the club second time around against Bournemouth at inside left.

Going back more than ten years or so no-one really talked about assists, but if they had during that time then Nicholas would have had a fair few to his credit. Indeed, it was Dai who created the through-ball for Jack Fowler that took Swansea into the quarter-finals of the FA Cup in 1926. But not content with stopping there, Nicholas also threaded through for Len Thompson to score the opening goal in the next-round victory over Arsenal that took the Swans into the semi-finals.

The following season saw Nicholas add 2 more caps to his Welsh collection against England and Northern Ireland but it was there that the collection stopped and, after six years at the Vetch, Nicholas left the club during the 1929/30 season.

Mel Nurse
1955-1962, 1968-1971

| League Appearances | 257 | League Goals | 12 |

Mel Nurse is another one of those people that if you cut them in half you would swear they would bleed black and white. After being affiliated to Swansea through their junior team, he signed his first professional contract for the club in June 1955. Already capped by Wales at Junior level, his form for Swansea led to him gaining more caps – first at Under-23 level and finally at full international level when he played against England at Wembley in 1960.

Nurse was an inspiration to Swansea during the late 1950s and early 1960s, despite the club struggling at times to maintain their Second Division status. The odd moment of glory – including a thirty-yard effort against Burnley in a FA Cup tie – was surrounded by too many occasions spent struggling and after several transfer requests the Swans eventually decided to agree. In 1962 he moved north to Ayresome Park, Middlesbrough.

He was to spend three seasons there – appointed captain soon after his arrival – before his wife wanted a return closer to home. However, during that time with Boro Mel scored a goal against the Swans that ironically sent them back into the Third Division at the end of the 1964/65 season. Three more seasons followed for Nurse at Swindon before he moved back to Swansea in the summer of 1968. In total he scored 11 goals in over 250 appearances for the club.

However, Mel Nurse and Swansea City were to re-form their partnership when Nurse was appointed to the board of the club under the regime of Silver Shield/Ninth Floor towards the end of the 1990s. As the club entered one of its bleakest spells, Nurse was instrumental in his efforts to remove unpopular owner Tony Petty at the end of 2001. Nurse also had a bar behind the North Bank named after him after he ploughed money into the club to refurbish the room and create the bar.

Jack O'Driscoll
1947-1952

| League Appearances | 118 | League Goals | 24 |

It's strange when you look through the record books of any football club to come across a player who has a career path that almost matches that of someone else. Indeed, if you look at Jack O'Driscoll in the record books then you could well be looking at the career of Rory Keane, such are the similarities between the two. As with Keane, O'Driscoll was brought to Swansea during the summer of 1947 for a fee of £3,000 from Cork. In his specialised position of outside right, O'Driscoll was gifted with great pace and one of the most powerful shots that Swansea fans had ever seen.

Jack was quick to establish himself in the Swansea side and was an integral part of the Championship-winning side of 1948/49. It was his crosses and forays down the wing that created the chances that were buried by Richards and McCrory up front. It was this kind of form that, like with Keane, led to international honours from both Northern and the Republic of Ireland – O'Driscoll won 3 caps for both sides during the late 1940s. O'Driscoll had caught the eye of Arsenal as well and Whittaker, their manager at the time, was present during the 1949/50 season to watch them play Luton. Although the Vetch directors stated that they were not 'inclined to sell' they did give Arsenal the first option on the player, along with Allchurch and Roy Paul.

O'Driscoll seemed set for bigger things and the top clubs were taking notice of his performances at the Vetch but, sadly for Jack, just as a move seemed inevitable he suffered an ankle injury that was to bring a premature end to his League career. O'Driscoll left the club at the end of the 1951/52 season having scored 26 times in 147 appearances for the club. Immediately after leaving the Vetch he moved to Llanelli for a spell.

Colin Pascoe
1983-1988, 1992, 1993-1996

| League Appearances | 270 | League Goals | 54 |

Colin Pascoe was just sixteen when the Swans won promotion to the First Division in 1981. It was a great time for the local lad from Port Talbot as he had just signed apprentice forms for the club as well, meaning that he was going to be an insider during the greatest adventure that the club ever had.

However, he had to wait two years for his League debut. That came in March 1983 when he appeared as a substitute for John Mahoney against Brighton. Before the 1982/83 season had finished, Pascoe had made his first full appearance in a Swansea shirt – away to Liverpool! Not a bad place to start a League career!

As the Swans slipped out of the First Division Pascoe became a first-team regular and, during the following season, he represented Wales at Under-21 level on four occasions. It was hard being a Swansea player during this period as the club slipped back down the road that took them up in the 1970s and Pascoe was at the club in December 1985 when it looked as if it was going to close. But he was one of the shining lights of that period and in 1986 he picked up his first Welsh cap when he appeared against Norway. Shortly before the Swans won promotion from the Fourth Division in 1988, Pascoe was on his way out of the Vetch to join Sunderland for £70,000. He had scored 45 goals in all competitions for the Swans in 201 appearances as he hit the road to the north east.

He was to make an immediate impact on Wearside, scoring on his first three appearances (against York, Chesterfield and Sunderland). The following season it was a Wembley appearance for Colin which ended in Sunderland losing the Second Division play-off final to Swindon. It seemed for all the world that he would miss out on the place in the First Division because of the defeat but Swindon were investigated for financial irregularities and demoted, and Sunderland took their place as runners-up in the play-off.

Pascoe was a hit at Sunderland, scoring 26 goals in 151 games for the club before he was loaned back to Swansea for a spell in 1992. Four goals in 17 games was enough for Pascoe to be brought 'back home' and he re-signed on a permanent basis in 1993. Three more years followed, including another appearance at Wembley, this time with a win over Huddersfield in the Autoglass Trophy final before he was released by the club in 1996 after suffering damage to his ankle ligaments. In total he had scored 65 goals for the club in 324 appearances. When he left Swansea he signed at Blackpool for a two-year spell but there was no going back and he managed just 1 game in that period.

Colin returned to the Vetch as part of the coaching staff during the 2004/05 season.

Roy Paul
1946-1950

| League Appearances | 159 | League Goals | 11 |

Roy Paul experienced his first taste of senior football when he appeared in a wartime League game for Swansea in 1939 but, due to the hostilities, football games came few and far between in the early part of his career. Paul was one of a group of players who progressed in the summer of 1939 – testament to the youth policy that had been started by Neil Harris.

But war ended in 1945 and Paul returned to the Vetch and won his Championship medal along with his teammates in 1948/49 when they lifted the Third Division (South) title. Indeed, Paul scored the most unusual goal of his career during this season. During one game, a cross from the right found Paul at the edge of the penalty area. He hurled himself forward and headed the ball into the net with tremendous force. Those that saw it agreed that he could not have hit the ball much harder with his foot. Also during the course of the season Paul was called upon to dispel a rumour that was circulating around Swansea. It said that there were problems in the dressing room and that fights had taken place between Swans players. Paul was adamant in public that the rumours were without foundation and the club issued a statement saying that they would take action against anyone who persisted in spreading them.

Roy Paul had received a taste of professional football and he was soon after heading off for Colombia in search of a fortune. He was to sign for Bogota. However, within two weeks of him leaving he was back home, professing himself 'disgusted with the situation'. After a meeting with the Swans' directors, he was placed on the transfer list. Within two weeks he was on his way to Manchester City for a fee 'in excess of £18,000'. The deal that took Paul to Maine Road was described by the City manager as the 'best he had ever done'.

Roy was equally successful at Manchester City and missed only one game during the 1950/51 season, a season that saw City return to the First Division. Two FA Cup finals followed during his City career and he was captain when they defeated Birmingham in the 1957 cup final. Paul's performances were also noted by Wales, with whom he won 33 international caps, 9 of which came from his spell at the Vetch.

Roy Paul was also the uncle of Alan Curtis – mentioned earlier in this book.

Cyril Pearce
1931-1932, 1937-1938

| League Appearances | 55 | League Goals | 43 |

Look in Swansea record books and you will still see the name of Cyril Pearce as the club's leading goalscorer in one season. Cyril joined the club at the start of the 1931/32 season from Newport County and made an immediate impact.

Pearce had joined a mediocre side, but that did not put him off as he found the net on a regular basis. By the end of October that season, the Swans had managed just ten points from thirteen games, yet Pearce had been on the scoresheet on seventeen occasions! With only half the season gone, Pearce was just 4 short of Fowler's record of 28 in a season. When you consider that at that stage no-one else had found the net on five occasions, it is tribute to Pearce's prowess in front of goal. Pearce's goalscoring exploits did at one stage lift the club to tenth in the League, a position from which they soon slipped. Pearce overtook Fowler's record with sixteen games to play, and on the day that he broke the record there were 14,000 people in the Vetch to see him do it.

Cyril was a natural goalscorer, as he proved by scoring 7 goals in the space of three days in 2 games at one stage during that season. Four were put past Notts County at the Vetch and three more at Port Vale during that spell. At the end of the season, Pearce had scored 35 goals, a record that still stands today. Unsurprisingly, this also earned Cyril the accolade of leading divisional goalscorer for the season.

Pearce's achievements on the pitch led to him moving to Charlton at the end of that season. Unlike previous heroes there was no massive outcry when Pearce was sold; it was almost as if the fans had got used to seeing their best players leave the club. He returned to the Vetch in 1937, where he played for one more year before his career finished due to injury. In total for the Swans he mustered 43 goals in just 56 games and, despite the shortness of his career at Swansea, he had made an impact that has withstood the test of time and his name remains firmly written in the history books of the Vetch.

Terry Phelan
1986-1987

| League Appearances | 45 | League Goals | 0 |

Terry Phelan played just 57 games for the Swans but during that period he became one of the most popular players at the Vetch. He began his professional career at Leeds United where he progressed right through the ranks to the first team, but his appearances were very limited and, after two years as a professional at Elland Road, he was released by the club. Terry Yorath, Swans' manager of the time, saw something he liked in Phelan and signed him in the summer of 1986 to play at left-back. Along with Tommy Hutchison, many Swans fans of the generation will remember

Hutchison jinking in and out of the people on the left-hand side of the Swans' midfield and Phelan providing the overlap with his electric pace.

Yorath was building for the future and, although the Swans finished twelfth during that season, Phelan had missed just one out of the forty-six league games and great things were expected of him the following season. He had not managed to hit the net for the Swans during his time at the Vetch but he had managed to score a particularly amusing own goal. With a ball coming towards Phelan in the box he stooped to head it out of play for a corner, but he completely misjudged it and the ball hit the back of his own net, to his bemusement.

Phelan, though, was to play no part in the Swans' promotion success of 1987/88 as Bobby Gould had signed him for Wimbledon during the close season. But while his old teammates were celebrating promotion the following summer, Phelan was celebrating his own success – the Dons' incredible FA Cup final victory over the giants of Liverpool. Phelan went on to play almost 200 games for the Dons before moving to Maine Road in 1992. Over 120 appearances followed there before he was surprisingly released by Manchester City and moved to Chelsea. Sadly for Phelan he never really established himself from that point onward and, despite spells with Everton, Crystal Palace, Fulham and Sheffield United, he brought a close to his career in 2002 with over 400 League appearances to his name.

Leighton Phillips
1978-1981

| League Appearances | 97 | League Goals | 0 |

Leighton Phillips began his career with Cardiff City and made an immediate impact on the club when he scored with his first ever touch for the team to help them to a draw with Rotherham United. However, it took him a little while to establish himself in the first team, but when he did his performances got him noticed and a series of Welsh caps at both Under-21 and Under-23 level followed, before he made his debut for the full national side against Czechoslovakia in 1971. In 1974 his performances were picked up by Aston Villa and, after 216 League outings for Cardiff, Phillips was on his way to Villa Park for the sum of £100,000.

While at Villa he helped them to win promotion to the First Division in 1975 as well as a League Cup winners' medal in 1977. Phillips arrived at the Vetch as one of the numerous people that Toshack was able to call upon as a contact and such was his pedigree, that Toshack parted with a then-club-record £70,000 to secure his services. He made his debut in November 1978 against Bury. The Swans won 1-0 with a side that was noticeable when you consider that no less than seven of the starting eleven had not been at the Vetch the previous season.

Phillips quickly made his presence felt and the Swans won promotion that season after lying in sixth place at the end of February. By the time April arrived, Swansea were top of the Third Division and Phillips was one of four players in the team at that time who received further international recognition from Wales. Phillips played his part in two seasons following that but, by the time the Swans won promotion to the First Division, he was out of favour at the Vetch and as Toshack prepared for life in the top flight in the summer of 1981 he decided that he was ready to listen to offers for Phillips. Considering just three years earlier the club had paid £70,000 to secure his services it seemed a very cut-down price when Phillips moved to Charlton for £25,000. However, it was explained at the time that the knock-down fee was as a result of the services that Phillips had given to the club and Phillips was eventually replaced by the ill-fated move for Colin Irwin.

Phillips only went on to make a few appearances for the Addicks before he saw out his playing days as a non-contract player with Exeter City. Leighton still lives and works in Swansea.

Ante Rajkovic
1980-1983, 1984

League Appearances 80 **League Goals** 2

Swansea already had one Yugoslav on the books when John Toshack decided that he needed another boost in the 1980/81 season and spent £100,000 of the club's money in Sarajevo to secure the services of international Ante Rajkovic. Rajkovic arrived at the Vetch with a reputation of being a very strong defender with the ability to read the game. He made his debut almost immediately in a goalless home draw with Bristol City at the Vetch but had severe fitness problems and this meant that he was restricted to just 1 more appearance before the end of that season.

As a result of the two Yugloslav players that the Swans had, they toured that country during the summer of 1981 but yet again Rajkovic was struck down with knee problems, meaning that he missed most of that tour. He recovered and took his place as sweeper in the Swans' defence as they embarked on their first season in the First Division. Many commentators during that 1981/82 season described Rajkovic as one of the best defenders in the English League. With the Swans playing a sweeper while no other teams tended to, Rajkovic was certainly an expert in this position and his international class clearly shone through for all that watched him during the course of the season. Rajkovic helped Swansea to a sixth-place finish that season as well as a place in the European Cup Winners' Cup through the triumph in the Welsh Cup final, and he was widely acclaimed by his opponents and colleagues as one of the top players in the division.

With the World Cup in Spain looming everyone was tipping Rajkovic to be in the Yugoslav squad but surprisingly he was omitted and he never really managed to scale the dizzy heights of that first full season again. In total he appeared 80 times in the League for the Swans before injury speeded up the end of his spell at the Vetch, and he left the club in 1983 as they were relegated back into the Second Division, a brief spell at the club in 1984 proved far less successful than the club and his association ended soon after.

Brayley Reynolds
1959-1964

| League Appearances | 150 | League Goals | 58 |

Brayley Reynolds started his football career with Lovells Athletic before joining Cardiff City in the summer of 1956. Reynolds was slightly smaller than your average centre forward but he did not allow that to deter him from scoring goals. In 54 League games for the Bluebirds he managed 15 goals for them before former Cardiff star Trevor Morris persuaded Brayley to join him at the Vetch. The transfer sum involved was described as a 'four-figure fee' although no exact figure was reported.

He continued his goal-scoring exploits for the Swans in his first season, notching 16 goals in 37 League appearances. That figure was eclipsed two years later when he managed 18 goals in 33 matches. On 24 April 1962, as the Swans flirted with relegation, they welcomed Plymouth Argyle to the Vetch. It was one of the team's finest performances and Reynolds was on fire that day as he grabbed his one and only Swans hat-trick in a 5-0 rout. There were just three games left to play at this stage and relegation had looked a sure-fire certainty until this result. Without taking too much away from the performance there were rumblings at the time that Plymouth had 'scratched the Swans' backs' as far as the result went.

In the next game, Swansea found themselves facing Sunderland. They drew 1-1 to ensure their safety. Reynolds was again on target as the celebrations started at the Vetch. They lasted long and hard as the following game saw Liverpool, the Champions, beaten 4-2. Swansea, and Reynolds in particular, had 'got out of jail'.

Brayley had scored 57 goals in 151 games when he left the club to play non-league football.

Stan Richards
1949-1950

| League Appearances | 62 | League Goals | 35 |

If you ever take a look at the results for the 1948/49 season, the name of Stan Richards will feature very prominently indeed as a goalscorer. Richards was brought up in south Wales but made his debut away in London with Tufnell Park before returning to play for Cardiff Corries. It was there that he was spotted by Billy McCandless, then in charge of Cardiff City, who wasted no time in snapping him up for them.

In his first season in blue Richards netted a then-club-record 30 goals in the season, but niggling injuries meant that his appearances in his second season were severely restricted and, with McCandless having moved on to Swansea, Richards followed him just in time for the Swans' Championship season. Richards, so it was said, had knees that were so bad that he could not train.

It was true that he did have considerable trouble with his knees but that did not hinder him as far as goal-scoring was concerned.

Richards netted 26 times in just 32 appearances for the club that season, including four in one game at the Vetch against Swindon. However, Richards was still suffering with his knee injuries and was forced to retire with 35 goals to his credit in a Swansea shirt from 65 games. It is safe to say that without his contribution, Swansea would not have managed one of their most successful seasons.

Jimmy Rimmer
1973-1974, 1983-1986

League Appearances   83   League Goals   0

Jimmy Rimmer won just about everything there was to win in football with medals such as the League Championship, European Cup and European Super Cup lining his trophy cabinet from his time with Aston Villa.

Rimmer started his career with Manchester United, with whom he won an FA Youth Cup winners' medal in 1964, before making his first-team debut for the Old Trafford outfit in 1967. However, he found himself consistently out of the side as an understudy for Alex Stepney. Harry Gregg, the then-Swansea manager and a former Manchester United goalkeeper himself, brought Rimmer to the Vetch in 1973 for a loan spell. Rimmer's game improved during the 17 games he played at the Vetch during that spell. Rimmer was widely credited with raising the confidence of other players at the Vetch during that time. He helped Swansea to a comfortable fourteenth place in the Fourth Division during his time at the Vetch and while the Swans weren't conceding many Rimmer was unable to help out at the other end, where the Swans only scored 3 goals in the last nine games of the season.

By the time he returned to Old Trafford his performances had been noticed and Arsenal paid Manchester United £40,000 for his services. During his time at Highbury he won a full England cap – against Italy in 1976 – and, after falling out with Gunners manager Terry Neill, he moved to Aston Villa. Villa went into a purple patch, following the 1981 League title with the European Cup in 1982 – a match that saw Rimmer injured very early on and Nigel Spink getting the main accolades for that performance. Spink's performance made him first-choice keeper at Villa Park and Rimmer returned to Swansea in August 1983. Times were very hard at the Vetch that season and a second successive relegation left them back in the Third Division. Indeed, if it was not for Rimmer the Swans would have been relegated three times in a row – but Rimmer kept them in the Third Division with a string of saves in a last-game 0-0 draw with Bristol City at the Vetch.

Rimmer retired from playing with a total of 83 League appearances under his belt for the club second time around and became youth team coach at the Vetch. When he finally left the club he opened a golf shop in the city.

Neil Robinson
1979-1984

| League Appearances | 123 | League Goals | 7 |

Neil Robinson joined the Swans in 1979 as they prepared for their first season back in the Second Division. It was the sum of £70,000 that persuaded Everton to part with the midfielder just two months into the new season. Robinson was one of several players that Toshack was bringing to the club at that time, with several others playing major parts in the next few years that would be so special to the club.

Neil had picked up a pre-season injury that season and his appearances were restricted to just 14 for the club during the following months, but that was enough to suggest that he would develop into a very useful midfield player. His place was consolidated in the following season and several more appearances followed during the course of the year that was to end with promotion to the First Division. Particularly as the season drew to a close, and it was between Swansea and Blackburn to take the final promotion spot behind West Ham and Notts County, did Robinson begin to shine. Robinson excelled as the Swans defeated Chelsea 3-0 at the Vetch in their penultimate home game of the season and, after a 2-2 draw against Luton in their last game, Robinson was named in the side to face Preston knowing that victory would take the Swans into the First Division. The Swans were already one up in front of their 10,000 travelling fans when Robinson crossed from the right to find Tommy Craig all too willing to slide the ball into the back of the net to put the Swans two ahead. With the eventual result being 3-1, Robinson had played a large part in securing the Swans' greatest promotion.

Robinson was also to feature quite heavily in the Swans' first season in the top flight and again played his own part in the success that they achieved that season. Indeed, Robinson scored his first League goal for the club during the course of the 1981/82 season. For almost two seasons, Neil Robinson found himself an almost certainty to be named in a Swans side. He only missed a few games here and there and, although not one of the shining stars of the teams of those days, he was certainly a very big part of the success that they achieved.

As the Swans went into their second season in the top flight, Robinson found his appearances restricted at the start of the season, although Toshack brought him back into the side on a regular basis in December as results went against the side. By the time March arrived, Robinson was back out of the side in favour of Chris Marustik as the Swans were relegated from the top flight.

William (Billy) Screen
1967-1972

| League Appearances | 142 | League Goals | 15 |

Billy Screen was born and bred in Swansea and made his debut for his hometown club against Aldershot in 1967, the year that Swansea played in the Fourth Division for the first time in their history. It was a hard time for Swansea when Screen made his debut, with the club struggling with finances and players needing to be sold just so that the books could be balanced.

It did not take long for Screen to show the Vetch Field faithful what the club had seen in him and, with his ability to tackle, the crowd soon took him to their hearts. His performances helped to ensure that the off-field problems did not materialise on the pitch and during his first season at the Vetch he helped the club into the fifth round of the FA Cup. Arsenal visited the Vetch and came away with a 1-0 victory in front of what still stands as a record Vetch Field crowd of 32,786 – almost ten times the crowd that watched the last home game of that season against Hartlepool.

It was not just the Swans fans that saw something they liked in Screen. His performances did not go unnoticed in Cardiff and he was capped twice at Under-23 level.

Screen helped the Swans to promotion in 1969/70 when they only lost seven games in finishing third in the division, and his performances were as solid as they had been throughout his career. Surprisingly, Screen was allowed to leave the Vetch in 1972 after 140 League games and 14 goals and he joined Newport County. He continued his career there for another four years, scoring 7 times in 142 League games before leaving League football for good.

Frank Scrine
1947-1953

| League Appearances | 142 | League Goals | 45 |

Had it not been for Adolf Hitler there is every chance that Frank would never have played for the Swans. As well as a being a competent footballer in his youth, Scrine was looking at a career in rugby but, with the outbreak of the Second World War and no rugby being played during that period, he reverted back to football.

After taking advice from a previous Swansea player, Jock Weir, Scrine was persuaded into a trial and he signed professional forms for the club in 1946. However, his debut was not imminent and he had to wait for his chance until October 1947 against Leyton Orient. Of course, being at the club at that time meant that Scrine was part of the successful Championship-winning side of 1948/49, and he managed a hat-trick during that season against Bristol Rovers. Scrine was described as a solidly built local boy with a tremendous body swerve. But the higher the level of football got, the better Scrine seemed to get as he excelled in the Swans' first season back in the Second Division and netted against Arsenal in the FA Cup as well as a hat-trick in the final of the Welsh Cup against Wrexham. This form was noticed and Scrine appeared twice for his country, with caps against England and Northern Ireland during 1950. During the course of the 1951/52 season, the Swans were in financial difficulties and there were several question marks raised over the value of transfers in and out of the club. It was during this period that Scrine, along with Reg Weston, asked to be transferred. Swansea finally decided to let him go in 1953, when he joined Oldham Athletic.

His Vetch career saw him net 45 times for the Swans in 142 League games and a further 21 goals followed at Oldham in 78 games.

Tommy Smith
1978-1979

League Appearances 36 **League Goals** 0

Tommy Smith was just a teenager when he was snapped up by Liverpool in the early 1960s. His first-team debut came in May 1963 when the Anfield outfit defeated Birmingham 5-1 in a League fixture. Smith was just eighteen at the time. He was soon established as one of the toughest defenders in the country but strangely he only won 1 England cap – against Wales in 1971.

Of course, he was part of the start of the Liverpool dynasty and in fifteen years as a professional at the club he won everything from the UEFA Cup to the European Cup. In total he played 632 games for the club and it is undoubted that his finest moment came when he scored Liverpool's second goal as they won their first European Cup in 1977. It was originally intended to be his last game in a Liverpool shirt but clearly the moment made him realise that he wanted one more season with the 'greatest club in the land'.

However, in the summer of 1978 he was finally on the move and he linked up with former clubmate John Toshack at Swansea. His debut in a Swans shirt came in a 3-0 win over Lincoln City at the Vetch. Smith was used just in front of the central defensive pairing of Nigel Stevenson and Stephen Morris. Despite staying at the Vetch for just one season few who were there will forget one particular game in which Smith played. The Swans had overcome Newport over two legs in the first round of the League Cup and were drawn against First Division Tottenham in the second round. Tottenham had just created history by signing two Argentineans – Ricky Villa and Osvaldo Ardiles – and few gave the Swans any chance of an upset. The game was not very old when Smith went in for a tackle on Ardiles and, to quote a saying I have heard many times, 'Ardiles flew ten feet in the air' – Smith had welcomed them to English football with a traditional challenge. It rattled Spurs and, despite them earning a replay after a 2-2 draw, Swansea were to upset the odds by winning the replay 3-1 at White Hart Lane.

As the season started to draw to a close, Smith's experience at the highest level was paying dividends and, along with Toshack, he bagged two goals in the destruction of Hull City. That result sparked a run in Swansea that was to lead to eventual promotion. Smith played 36 games in that season with the two goals against Hull being the only time he found the net. But in October 1979 he gave in to persistent knee problems and his contract was cancelled by mutual consent. He returned to Liverpool for a short spell on the coaching staff before retiring from football completely. Tommy now commentates on local radio in Liverpool.

Nigel Stevenson
1975-1987

League Appearances 257 **League Goals** 15

Nigel Stevenson joined Swansea as a schoolboy and was with the club right through the promotions from the Fourth to the First Division and then back again – not bad for a spell that only lasted twelve years!

It was around the time that Harry Griffiths was looking for players elsewhere when Stevenson was in the youth team with two more home-grown products, Stephen Morris and Jeremy Charles. Griffiths was struggling to get people to come to the Vetch from elsewhere so he took the chance on youth and Stevenson made his debut for the club against Southport in 1976. During the course of the 1979/80 season Swansea were drawn with Tottenham in the League Cup. Toshack made the decision to field Stevenson and Morris together at the centre of defence and both played out of their skins against their illustrious opponents to help Swansea to a well-deserved 2-2 draw. Stevenson played 31 games during the course of that season and it was recognised within the club that he was working hard to improve himself.

Stevenson, like so many of the players he grew up with, celebrated his finest achievement on 2 May 1981 when he took the field against Preston and played his part in a 3-1 victory that took Swansea back into the top flight. However, Toshack was not convinced that Stevenson was up to the demands of First Division football and bought Colin Irwin from Liverpool to plug the gap that he felt was there. Stevenson, though still only twenty-two, was not to be put off and he won back his place in the side. By the end of that first season in the top flight it was recognised that, while

Stevenson may not have been one of the real 'stars' of the Swansea side, he was a superb advert for all young players that hard work and dedication brings its own rewards. During the 1981/82 season he was rewarded with the first of 4 Welsh caps when he played against England at Ninian Park.

Swansea offered him a testimonial match after ten seasons at the Vetch and John Toshack brought back his Real Sociedad side to take on Swansea. Stevenson, though, was coming to the end of his Swansea career and he was loaned out shortly after the testimonial to both Cardiff City and Reading. Speedy eventually left the Vetch in the summer of 1987 when he joined Cardiff. Sixty-eight League appearances followed for the Bluebirds before he finally brought the curtain down on his career. Stevenson now works for Royal Mail in Swansea.

Joe Sykes
1924-1935

| League Appearances | 314 | League Goals | 7 |

Joe Sykes had begun his League career with Sheffield Wednesday but struggled to establish himself in the Hillsborough side – making just 28 League appearances in a five-year spell with the club. In the summer of 1924 he decided to move clubs and was persuaded by Swansea manager Joe Bradshaw to move to south Wales. It had been reported that Liverpool had offered £3,000 for Sykes' services but the Owls had refused to sell. No-one indicated what the club had paid for Sykes but the rumours were that it must have been significantly more than this figure.

He made his debut at centre half for the club in a 2-0 win over Merthyr during the 1924/25 season, having replaced the injured Jimmy Collins in the Swansea side. Sykes was not the tallest of men, standing at just 5ft 9in, but he very rarely lost a ball in the air and it was widely acknowledged that his timing was immaculate and his passing superb. Indeed, in the papers Sykes was described as 'brainy', had 'clever anticipation' and 'carpet passes'. The fans were in agreement with the press and had taken Sykes to their hearts. It looked like the start of a long and fruitful partnership.

By the time November 1924 had arrived Sykes was appointed as captain for the game against Brentford and the Swans ran out 7-0 winners. At the end of his first season with the club, Sykes had led them to their first Third Divison (South) Championship, having been beaten just eight times during the course of the season. Sykes was highlighted in the AGM at the end of the 1928/29 season as someone who had given sterling work on and off the pitch for the club. This was testament to the way that Sykes was conducting himself within the club and the respect that he had from colleagues and fans alike.

In the 1933/34 season Sykes appeared in just 2 games as the Swans narrowly avoided relegation and, at the end of the following season, he decided that he was too old to continue playing and retired from the club. 'The diminutive giant' who could 'out-jump a man a foot taller' would be sadly missed on the pitch for Swansea, but his presence within the club was far from finished.

At the end of the Second World War Sykes was back as assistant trainer to Frank Barson, who had just arrived at the Vetch with the reputation as a hard man. In 1953 the Swansea directors wanted McCandless to train the players more, but Billy was more than happy to let Sykes take this aspect on his own. In fact it is Sykes who is credited with spotting Ivor Allchurch playing on a public park and bringing him to the club as a fifteen-year old. At the end of the 1954/55 season, Sykes was presented with a gift by some of the players that he had nurtured through the system 'in appreciation of the great help', which was just reward for the man who gave his all.

When Billy McCandless died before the 1955/56 season started, Sykes was appointed, along with Ivor Allchurch and Ron Burgess (team manager), onto the three-man team selection committee. At the end of the 1959/60 season he was appointed as assistant manager to Trevor Morris as the backroom staff at the Vetch was switched around.

After a terrible start to the 1966/67 season, the Swans parted company with manager Glyn Davies and appointed Sykes as caretaker manager, over forty years since he first joined the club. Despite putting some results together to give a glimmer of hope, Sykes and eventual new manager Billy Lucas were unable to stop the slide and the Swans slipped into the Fourth Division.

When Leeds arrived at the Vetch to play in Ivor Allchurch's testimonial in May 1968 the great man himself paid tribute to Joe Sykes, who had discovered him all those years ago playing park football. Sykes himself recalled that Ivor 'only had to touch the ball once for me to realise he could be a great player'. Sykes, then aged seventy-one, resigned from the club in June 1968 after forty-four years with the club. Many were quick to praise the man that had served the club with such great distinction and it was widely accepted that the Vetch would be a lesser place without him.

As Swansea entered one of their darkest phases in 1974/75, it was announced that Joe Sykes had died. He was immediately missed and mourned by all connected with Swansea and maybe it was some of the spirit that he injected into the club that saved it from relegation at the end of the season. Joe Sykes was quite simply one of the greatest players and people ever to grace the Vetch Field.

Geoff Thomas
1965-1976

| League Appearances | 357 | League Goals | 52 |

Ten seasons were spent at the Vetch by Geoff Thomas, who was a product of the Swans' youth system. He made his debut at the start of the 1965/66 season in midfield, a position that he was to hold for most of his Swansea career. Very rarely did he miss a game and, because of this, he grew to become a rock that a generation of Swans' players looked up to.

Geoff never gained full honours for Wales but he was capped three times at Under-23 level for his country. He did manage to achieve two hat-tricks for the club – one against Grimsby and the other against Doncaster Rovers. Strangely enough, they were the only two hat-tricks scored by Swansea players during a period of very nearly two years.

As he got older, Thomas was pushed back into defence but it was a move that never really proved successful and he left Swansea having scored 52 goals in over 360 games for the club.

Len Thompson
1922-1928

| League Appearances | 188 | League Goals | 89 |

Len Thompson joined the Swans in the summer of 1922 from Birmingham along with his friend and strike partner Harry Deacon. Having previously had spells with Sheffield and Barnsley before joining Birmingham, Thompson had won England Schoolboy honours before the outbreak of the First World War. Along with Deacon, Thompson was quick to establish himself in a side that was improving season on season and this culminated with the Third Division (South) Championship win of 1924/25. Indeed, during that season many a defence struggled to cope with the skills of Thompson – least of all Brentford, who conceded four goals to the man in a 7-0 drubbing at the Vetch, Harry Deacon grabbing the other three goals in that particular encounter. Thompson, though, missed a couple of games towards the end of this season through injury and had to watch from the sidelines as Billy Whitehead replaced him. However, he was back in the side when Exeter arrived on the last day of the season. A win was needed to secure the title and Thompson grabbed the crucial second goal as the side won 2-1.

The following season was another incredible one for Thompson as the Swans reached the semi-finals of the FA Cup. Thompson also managed to set a record for the time. During a League match against Wolves, a match that Swansea were to go on to win 3-2, Thompson found the back of the net after just ten seconds.

The following season was Thompson's most successful in a Swansea shirt with 26 goals to his name, but that was to be his last full season in the shirt as a knee injury kept him out of action at the start of the next season. Shortly after that Swansea sold Thompson to Arsenal for the sum of £4,000, with 86 goals in 187 appearances for the Swans under his belt. Thompson had first come to the attention of Arsenal when three of their scouts watched him have an 'outstanding game' against Luton at the Vetch in 1925. Despite the Gunners announcing their representatives were watching Luton players, Thompson must have impressed them sufficiently even though the move took three years to materialise.

However, despite becoming a favourite at Highbury for his penalty-taking ability, Thompson was forced to retire from playing football in 1933 due to a recurrence of the knee injury that he first experienced when playing at the Vetch.

John Toshack
1978-1981, Manager 1978-1984

| League Appearances | 63 | League Goals | 25 |

John Toshack was already a legend in Welsh football before he ever arrived at Swansea City. A product of the back streets of Cardiff, he had made his debut for the Bluebirds aged just sixteen. For those that saw Toshack, you will not be surprised to hear that he scored in that game and the legend was born.

Toshack's exploits did not stop there as he finished the leading goalscorer in the Second Division during the 1968/69 season. More goals followed over the course of the next season-and-a-half before Bill Shankly decided to part with £110,000 of Liverpool's money to take Toshack to Anfield. As Shankly began to build the Liverpool dynasty that dominated the British scene for almost twenty years, Toshack built an understanding with Kevin Keegan. Scoring around a goal every other game, Toshack was also responsible for many of Keegan's goals with his ability to head the ball into the path of his partner, who would bury the chance. As the 1970s passed the midway mark, Toshack found himself increasingly out of the Liverpool side through injury and in February 1978 he took the chance to step into management at Swansea, overlooking the chance of a possible return to Ninian Park along the way. As he arrived at the Vetch with UEFA Cup, FA Cup and League Championship medals, he became the youngest manager in the Football League.

Swansea had narrowly missed out on promotion the year before Toshack arrived, but he made immediate amends for that and took them straight out of the Fourth Division with a victory on the last day of the season. The following season, Toshack the player helped the Swans with a goal against Chesterfield that sealed a return to the Second Division. Consolidation was the name of the game the next season but on 2 May 1981, just over three years after his arrival, Toshack took Swansea to their highest ever position as the Swans triumphed 3-1 at Preston.

But Tosh wasn't done and Swansea ended their first season in the top flight in sixth place, their lowest position during that season and, indeed, until within around six weeks of the season ending there was even talk that the Swans could be crowned League Champions. Of course, as with most things Swansea City, that 1981/82 season was not without its ironies. The biggest one as far as Toshack was concerned was his first return to Anfield, later in 1981. Bill Shankly had remained a big influence on Toshack's career while he learned his trade in management at Swansea and Toshack looked forward to leading his side out at Anfield knowing that Shankly would be as proud as he was. But fate was to play its part and Shankly died just a few days before the fixture was played. It was with great emotion on Toshack's part that he stood in front of the Kop for the minute's silence wearing his Liverpool number 10 shirt as a tribute to the man who had taught him so much.

Toshack's exploits at Swansea were rewarded with an MBE in the New Year's Honours list in 1982 and also an appearance on the BBC programme This is Your Life. His time at Swansea turned sour when the club was relegated at the end of the 1982/83 season and in October 1983 he resigned as manager of Swansea City. Two months later the directors of the club invited him back but it was to last just four months and in March 1984 he made his final departure from the Vetch.

After he left Toshack was appointed manager at some of the biggest teams in European football. He had spells at Sporting Lisbon, Real Sociedad and Real Madrid. He spent one year in charge at Madrid but, despite delivering the League Title, he was sacked. Sociedad beckoned again before he succeeded Terry Yorath as Welsh team manager. Toshack bore the brunt of the backlash from the departure of Yorath and just forty-four days later he left the job after just one game in charge.

85

A return to Spain quickly followed where Toshack managed both Deportivo La Coruna and, for a second time, Real Madrid.

Toshack was appointed as Welsh manager for a second time during 2004 with the goal to qualify for the European Championships in 2008 after Wales had a disastrous start to qualifying for World Cup 2006. As a result he is often seen watching the Swans and took part in the celebrations of the last League game at the Vetch Field.

Lee Trundle
2003–Present

League Appearances 73 (to end 2004/2005 season)   **League Goals** 39 (to end 2004/2005 season)

Few players can lay claim to the amount of media coverage that Lee Trundle has gained since he arrived at Swansea in the summer of 2003, joining up with former manager Brian Flynn at the Vetch on a free transfer. Trundle has featured weekly on cult soccer programme Soccer AM, with numerous other pundits singing his praises for his trickery and showboating skills. In addition to that he was named in the FA Cup team of the season in 2004 as well as being awarded the Powerade Player of the Season for League Two in 2005.

Trundle was first spotted by Brian Flynn while playing for Rhyl and, in 2001, at the age of twenty-five, he was persuaded to turn professional with Wrexham. Eight goals followed in his first 14 games for the Robins and that was followed by 10 the following season and 12 the season after – a season that saw Wrexham promoted and Trundle playing a major part in the 35 goals for Andy Morrell, his strike partner. However, Wrexham had allowed his contract to run out and when Brian Flynn became aware of his availability there was only one place for Lee to head. That was Swansea, to join up with the man who gave him his chance in League football.

It is his skills that have made Trundle a firm favourite among the Swansea crowd, as well as his scoring of over 40 goals in his first two seasons at the club in all competitions. Trundle's first came on his debut against Bury in August 2003 and they have flowed at regular intervals since then, including two hat-tricks – away to Cheltenham and home to Notts County.

Trundle does have his critics and was lambasted by Huddersfield manager Peter Jackson, who saw Trundle roll the ball around his shoulders against his side at the Vetch in 2003 – one of several moments of showmanship that he has undertaken in his time at Swansea. In 2005, Trundle became the first Swansea player for over twenty years to notch 20 League goals in a season and with his place assured in Swansea legend he is almost certain to add to his goal tally in the seasons to come. He will quite probably earn the first 'legend' tag of the new stadium. A showboating genius and a massive asset to the club to boot.

Alan Waddle
1978-1980. 1985-1986

| League Appearances | 127 | League Goals | 43 |

Alan Waddle began his career as a centre forward with Halifax before Bill Shankly decided that he could do a job for him at Liverpool and, in the summer of 1973, he was on his way to Anfield. However, he found it very difficult to get into the side at Liverpool, thanks mainly to the form of both Kevin Keegan and his strike partner John Toshack. Just 22 appearances followed in the four years he spent there. His only goal came in December 1973 when he poked home an Ian Callaghan cross to defeat Everton at Goodison Park. His last game for the club was in the European Cup semi-final against FC Zurich in 1977 before he was transferred back to his place of birth – Leicester.

But again it wasn't to be a successful move and just eight months later he was back with Toshack at Swansea. Toshack paid the Filbert Street outfit £24,000 to secure the services of Waddle – someone who he knew from their time together could do a very good job for the club. Waddle indeed did make an immediate impact at the club by being named the fans' Player of the Year for his 19 goals, which included a hat-trick in a 3-2 home victory over Southend with just three games to go. Waddle wasn't finished there though. He was also to net, in the last game of the season, the equaliser in a 2-1 victory over Chesterfield at the Vetch.

Toshack's faith in Waddle had been repaid and the Swans were back in the Second Division with no shortage of debt to the big man. He helped consolidate the Swans' position in the Second Division the following season but, by the time the 1980/81 season was halfway through, Newport had paid £80,000 to take Waddle on. Moves in quick succession followed to Mansfield, Hartlepool (twice) and Peterborough before he found himself back at the Vetch in March 1985. The following season saw the club as a whole in the dumps as they were wound up and saved at the eleventh hour from extinction. Waddle hung up his boots at the end of the 1985/86 season. He scored 44 league goals in total for the Swans – the most productive total that he managed at any of his clubs.

Keith Walker
1989-2000

| League Appearances | 268 | League Goals | 9 |

Keith Walker had already played for both Stirling Albion and St Mirren before switching to south Wales in 1989 and an eleven-year stint with Swansea. When he joined it was as part of a trio of Scottish players that had been brought in – Paul Chalmers and John Hughes being the other two. Quickly nicknamed 'Sky' by the Swansea supporters, out of the three players he was the one that settled in the quickest and, despite a series of injuries, he was a regular in the Swansea side.

After Swansea won the Autoglass Trophy in 1994, he underwent his third hernia operation and was unable to command a regular place because every time he settled he seemed to receive another injury setback. At the start of the 1997/98 season he was appointed as club captain by Jan Molby and became a legend in Swansea when he scored the winning goal against Cardiff City at Ninian Park in front of the live Sky Television cameras. It was a traumatic time at Swansea as Jan Molby, Mickey Adams and Alan Cork all sat in the managerial hot seat during the course of that season and the Swans finished far too low down the Football League for their own liking.

Walker was forced to sit out most of the next two seasons at the club due to injury as Swansea first missed out in the play-offs before securing the Division Three Championship in 2000. That season saw 'Sky' being awarded a testimonial season, which culminated in a game against Aston Villa at the Vetch. While Swans fans first believed that it would be a celebration of the Championship secured at Rotherham just a few days before, it turned into a mourning for the loss of one of their fans at that game. Sky though was well rewarded and, although he had left the club by that stage, Swansea fans payed tribute with one last rendition of 'You'll never beat Keith Walker'.

Keith went immediately into management with Merthyr Tydfil and many expected to see him back at the Vetch in charge one day but, soon after his retirement, he left Merthyr and returned to his native Scotland. He joined Strathclyde police force after citing family reasons behind his decision to leave Wales.

Reg Weston
1946-1952

| League Appearances | 229 | League Goals | 1 |

Reg Weston was a player with Northfleet in March 1945 when Swans manager Haydn Green decided to bring him to the Vetch Field. The centre half was designed as someone who could tighten up the Swans' defence as they prepared for football again after the war period.

By the time the 1948/49 season arrived Reg was the captain of the side and just the second Swans captain to experience success in the League as they won the Third Division (South) Championship at the end of the season. Promotion was secured on 15 April 1949 when the Swans beat Newport 2-1 at the Vetch and, as the crowd celebrated the success on the pitch at the end of the game, Weston addressed them from the grandstand, with most being fully aware that the Championship was within one point of being clinched. A win at Brighton in the next game secured that feat. At a dinner to celebrate the Championship shortly after the season finished, Weston was singled out for extra praise by the lord mayor, Williams A. Jenkins, who stated that he was 'a fine leader, sportsman and person'.

Weston was instrumental in some of the records that were broken by the Swans that season, records that included seventeen home wins and an unbeaten record at the Vetch. With the Swans back in the Second Division, Weston found himself a virtual ever-present over the course of the next two seasons, with only the occasional match seeing Tom Kiley needed to replace him.

The Swans had just completed their third season in the Second Division when Weston's contract was due for renewal. Weston asked the Swansea board for assistance in overcoming a housing problem but the board refused to help him. Weston refused on that basis to re-sign and left the club. He may not have been someone that set the world alight during his time at the Vetch but he had certainly been a tower of strength for the Swans during his seven years. His straightforward style had complemented those around him and he was classed as an honest man who never undersold himself or his colleagues.

After leaving the Vetch, Weston headed for Derby County, although he never made a first-team appearance for the Rams.

Walter Whittaker

Player and Manager 1912-1914

Walter Whittaker was Swansea's first manager, having been appointed in July 1912. He was chosen from a shortlist of three people for the job, the others being Ben Hall (Derby County) and W. Annan (Bristol City). Walter was given just eight weeks to build himself a team before the club's first match. Arrivals had to come quickly and Whittaker wasted no time in bringing Ball, Coleman and Emerson into the club as the start of his team.

Walter built Swansea Town from scratch. Not just players either; one of his roles was also to supervise the building of the Vetch Field, which we now know as the former home of the football club. It appeared that his talents would run far and wide and 2,000 people turned up to watch one of the trial matches on the town's recreation ground, describing the play as bright and open.

He immediately found that his team were challenging for success on the pitch. His first season saw Swansea crowned as not only winners of the Welsh League but also the Welsh Cup. They missed out on promotion from the Southern League Second Division and the completion of a remarkable hat-trick, but Walter's leadership had proved that the club had arrived with a bang and were determined to make a mark on the football ladder. Chairman J.W. Thorpe thanked Walter publicly for all he had done for the club in this incredible start to life.

One of the strange things that Walter had to put up with in those days was the fact that the directors, not the manager, picked the team. This was highlighted on the eve of the Swans' debut in the first round of the FA Cup when it was reported that the directors did not meet until 2.30 p.m. on the Friday to select the team for this historic occasion.

At the end of the 1913/14 season, the Swans had been reasonably successful. They had finished their second season fourth in the Southern League and second in the Welsh League. Football had been established in Swansea. However, it was not enough and Walter was surprisingly sacked from his position as manager. The papers reported it as a 'great shock to all Swansea' but there were rumblings that it was a change in the views of the board.

Whittaker's relative success was made all the more remarkable when you consider that he was also a player for the club during those two years – keeping goal with some athleticism. For those first two years Walter set the foundations for the club that we know now and for that he will never be forgotten.

Herbie Williams

1958-1975

| League Appearances | 489 | League Goals | 103 |

Herbie Williams had an association with football in Swansea that lasted twenty years. He started as a member of the Swansea Schoolboys side that won the English Schools trophy and the Welsh Shield in 1954. The following year they retained the Welsh Shield – this time with Williams as captain.

He was working at Swansea docks when Swansea offered him professional terms and, at the age of seventeen, he was thrown into the first team to make his debut in a 5-0 win over Sunderland. Williams was part of the Swansea side that made it through to the semi-finals of the FA Cup in 1964 before losing 2-1 to Preston at Villa Park. The following season he won the first 2 of his 3 Welsh caps when he played twice against Greece – although it was seven years before he was to win the third, against Romania.

When Roy Bentley was appointed as manager of Swansea in 1969 he appointed Herbie Williams as his captain, Williams celebrating with the rest of his teammates as they won promotion at the end of the following season.

Williams played in a total of 513 League games for the Swans and under a total of seven managers – possibly not a bad total in the world of modern football. He scored on 104 occasions before leaving the Vetch in January 1975 to pursue a new life in Australia.

Ronnie Williams
1929-1935, 1936-1939

| League Appearances | 185 | League Goals | 51 |

Ronnie Williams signed for the Swans in 1929 and made one of the most eventful debuts in the club's history. The Swans were bottom of the Second Division when manager James Thompson decided that he would try the young Williams at centre half. Ronnie was the sixth person that had been tried in that position during the early part of that season but he proved to be an instant success as he hit a hat-trick. Because of this start to his career it naturally didn't take Williams long to establish himself as a favourite with the Swansea supporters and, by the end of his first season with the club, he was the top scorer.

This was a feat that he managed to repeat during the course of the 1930/31 season, during which he scored his second hat-trick, on 22 November at home to Nottingham Forest. Injury then started to blight his career with the Swans but, shortly after he had scored his fiftieth League goal in a Swansea shirt, he joined Newcastle United.

Williams was a hard man for Swansea to replace and his career moved on slowly at Newcastle although it did lead to him gaining caps for Wales when he appeared against both Scotland and England in 1935. Williams only went on to play 36 games for the St James' Park outfit, during which he scored 14 goals, including three in a 7-3 victory over Everton at Goodison Park. Williams did return to the Vetch for a brief spell but was unable to produce the same kind of form as he did before he left.

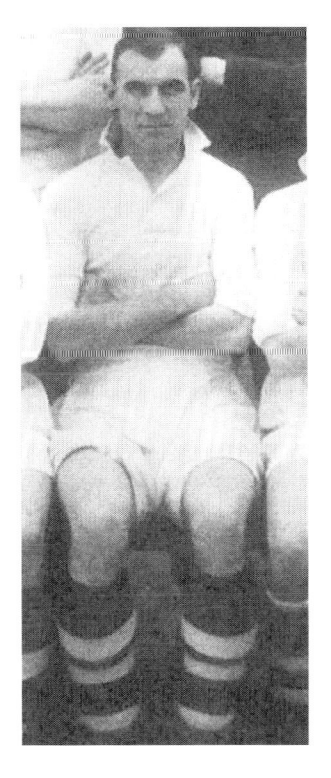

Arthur Willis
1954-1957

League Appearances   98   League Goals   0

Arthur Willis was working down the mines when he was discovered by Tottenham Hotspur and was offered the chance to go to White Hart Lane. He made his debut for the club during the Second World War and during that period he was offered professional terms. He found himself a regular in the full-back position at the Lane until 1947, when he lost his place to Sid Tickridge.

However, Willis was not to be dismissed out of hand by Spurs and he worked hard on his game and eventually was rewarded by regaining his position during the course of the 1949/50 season. He won a League Championship with Spurs as part of their legendary 'push and run' side and was capped for England when he played against France in October 1951.

In total he played in 161 games for Spurs before he left the club. At the age of thirty-four he found himself on the move, joining his former teammate Ron Burgess at the Vetch Field. Swansea paid £3,000 to secure his services and knew that, as a stylish player, he would fit well into the flowing type of football that the club was playing. His debut for the club came a few days later against Liverpool, a match that the club won 3-2, but the joy was short-lived as his second appearance saw the Swans defeated 7-0 at Eastville against Bristol Rovers.

Willis helped the club to the Welsh Cup final in 1956 before being appointed onto the coaching staff at the club. He left Swansea in 1960 while on the coaching staff, a summer that saw the club decimated with departures. After leaving the Vetch he joined Welsh League club Haverfordwest as player-manager before retiring from the game permanently.

And Finally...

I feel it only appropriate to end this book with just a short piece on the players that came so very close to being included in it. It was a tough job to narrow down to just 100 players but we managed it in the end after discussion, debate and good old-fashioned disagreements.

You only have to think of players like Christian Edwards and Steve Jenkins to know who we are thinking of. They were players that went onto bigger and better things – testament to the skills that they learned while they were here. Mark Harris and Martin Thomas are both players that we remember for one reason or another. You are now getting some idea of how hard we had to work just to come up with the final list that we used.

Of course there were others that brought First Division football to the club that we didn't mention. The likes of Dave Stewart and David Giles made that dream of twenty years ago all possible. Going back further into our history we remember other people who brought us success that we have left out – the likes of Keith Todd and Eddie Thomas.

Look at other people as well. Brian Flynn saved us from being relegated from the Football League when it looked nigh on impossible, and who could ever forget that magical day in May 2003 when James Thomas scored a hat-trick to secure League football? We remember as well people like Joe Allon, who equalled the club record of scoring in consecutive games, and maybe even Walter Boyd and his distinction of being sent off after 0 seconds.

No doubt some of you have your favourites who are not included in this book, and for that we apologise, but we knew it was going to happen. We are not saying these are the 100 greatest Swansea players/managers – just 100 greats who have graced this club.

To those we have missed out we thank you for your part in the history of this club and to those that are in here we salute each and every one of you. As Swansea City move forward in their new home and a new era opens, we feel it only fitting to close the old one having given you 100 Swansea greats. Who will make up the 100 Swansea greats of the new era? You'll have to wait and see, but those on the following pages are strong contenders...

Jason Scotland

| League Appearances | 95 | League Goals | 51 |

Jason signed for Swansea City at the start of the 2007/08 season from St Johnstone and made an immediate impact at the Liberty Stadium from day one. The small fee paid for the Trinidad and Tobago International player became the best bit of business that manager Roberto Martinez could have done, as Scotland scored time and time again during his first season, lifting Swansea City into a Championship play-off place on three occasions. His first season saw him hit the back of the net 27 times in a total of 47 appearances using his extreme strength when back to goal to punish the very best the league had to offer. In his second season he again set the league alight scoring 24 goals in 48 appearances. Premier League clubs were beginning to circle, and when Roberto Martinez left the Liberty for Wigan Athletic it was only a matter of time before he raided his old club for their star striker. In a £2 million deal Scotland left Swansea on 20 July 2009 for Lancashire. He never found his true scoring form in the Premier League, netting only twice in 18 appearances. He eventually went on loan and then signed on a free deal at Ipswich Town. For two seasons Jason Scotland set the Liberty Stadium on fire setting scoring records and forever has a place in Swansea hearts. His 'Caribbean' style of play and sometimes lethargic attitude to his craft may well have annoyed some supporters, but when the stats are reviewed Jason Scotland was as good a player as any Swans fan could have seen over the past 98 years. Simply a goal scoring machine. Simply – Jason Scotland.

Darren Pratley

Barking-born Darren joined Swansea City for £100,000 from Fulham in 2006 after a relatively decent spell on loan at Brentford. Initially he found it difficult to find his feet at the club. Seen by some as a negative midfielder, he blossomed into a strong and athletic player under the guidance of Roberto Martinez, and has been a regular choice to the present day. When Darren Pratley plays well, Swansea City play well, and when he probes forward, either scoring with late runs into the box or from distance, he is the team's talisman. Called up for Jamaica by John Barnes in 2009 he withdrew from the squad through injury. If Darren's aspirations are matched by Swansea City that may well go in his favour as the club are pushing for promotion to the Premier League in 2011. An England cap will no doubt follow if he maintains his desire to be at the top of his game and Swansea are again in the top league. However, in recent times a line of clubs have tried to sign him, making what would be considered derisory offers for such a talent. His contract is up at Swansea in May 2011, and only then will we see where Darren Pratley plays. When all is considered he is a Premier League player and many at the Liberty will hope that that will be with Swansea City. He broke the 150 game mark for the Swans in December 2010 with a return of approximately 1 goal in 5 games, netting twice in yet another derby victory against Cardiff City in November 2009.

Garry Monk

Garry struggled to find his true home until he signed for the Swans in June 2004, and he is now fast approaching 200 games for the club. It could be said that after stints at Torquay United, Southampton, Stockport, Oxford, Sheffield Wednesday and Barnsley he was fast becoming a lower league journeyman. However that would change, as under the guidance of Kenny Jackett and then Roberto Martinez, Monk has shone at the heart of the Swansea City defence. A solid and uncompromising player who reads the game extremely well, he relies on an athletic stature to command and captain the blood line of the team. The European style of play adored by the Swansea faithful has not been a problem for Garry as he plays the ball out of defence time and time again to feet ready for the next Swansea free-flowing attack. He has been at the club as they have progressed through the lower leagues to a challenge at the top of the Championship in 2011. At times suffering from annoying injuries, he has always bounced back to become one of the supporters' favourite players, giving back to a club the faith that they have shown in him game after game. When Garry hangs up his boots he will be one of the most difficult players to replace. He is like Mark Harris – Mr Swansea City – adored by the city and hated by many a centre forward. An intelligent footballer, and some would say good enough to make a Premier League team, he has a found a home in Swansea, and he may well join the many players to settle and live out their days on the real South Wales coast in West Glamorgan.

Alan Tate

Once a Manchester United and Royal Antwerp player, Alan Tate found his football home when he signed for the Swans properly on 6 February 2004 after two successful loan spells from Manchester United. In the past three seasons, Tate has excelled and blossomed into a loyal Swansea servant earning him a place in many fans' hearts as a tough defender, midfielder, striker and goalkeeper. 'A team of Alan Tates' is what some Swans fans dream about – his commitment and desire to win at any cost is what all supporters of a club want to see. Cautioned for a public order offence with Lee Trundle when he held up a Welsh flag after a Millennium Stadium cup victory against Carlisle in April 2006 citing a 'dislike' for Cardiff City, this event alone made him a hero in some Swansea hearts. But on the field his performances, character and at times fearless approach will be what he is remembered for. Placing his body on the line in yet another Swansea victory at Cardiff in November 2010 as the stadium jeered and booed him, proved to all jacks that he is one of the very few players in British football who is loyal, proud and excited to serve the city's club. When a Swansea all time eleven is drawn up he will get into the team based on his lion heart and solid Durham-born grit. He is a battling, tough player who fears nothing and loves the club and its supporters like no other in recent times. And yes, he has kept a clean sheet when playing in goal when called upon versus QPR in the 2008/09 season. Indeed – a team of Alan Tates may well exist.

When a choice is made by any author about who should and who should not be included in any dream collection of players, there will always be conversation and comment. An updated Leon Britton and Angel Rangel could claim a spot in this update as could players like Nathan Dyer, Scott Sinclair or Ashley Williams. But they are for the future, and for now this is the updated best! And they ain't that bad at all…

Other sports titles published by The History Press

Newport County Football Cub 1912-1960
RICHARD SHEPHERD

From its formation in 1912 to the departure of Bill Lucas as manager in 1960, Newport County Football club has a proud yet often troubled history. This book explores the part played by employees of Lysaght's Works in the club's beginnings, the roles of the early managers and the development of teams built for success in the 1930s. Promotion from the third division, the post war years and some memorable FA Cup matches are all here in a collection of over 250 photographs and memorabilia.

0 7524 1081 4

Cardiff City Football Club 1971-1993
RICHARD SHEPHERD

This collection of action shots, team groups and player portraits looks at the history of Cardiff City Football Club from 1971, when the Bluebirds narrowly missed out on First Division football, to 1993 when a resurgence of interest following the backing of Barry-based businessman Rick Wright saw Eddie May's squad take the Division Three title and the Welsh Cup with the likes of Robbie James, Carl Dale, Phil Stant and Nathan Blake. All the highs and lows of twenty-two years are in these pages with expert captions by Welsh football historian Richard Shepherd.

0 7524 2068 2

Swansea Rugby Football Club Since 1945
BLEDDYN HOPKINS

During the period since 1945 many famous players have represented the 'All Whites', including Haydn Tanner, 'Billy' Williams, Clem Thomas, Dewi Bebb, Mervyn Davies, David Richards, Geoff Wheel, Robert Jones, the Moriarty brothers (Paul and Richard), Garin Jenkins and Scott Gibbs, and no less than sixty-five players from the club have been capped by Wales during this period. In the light of the most recent Welsh rugby reorganization, the book assumes added significance as Swansea Rugby Football Club emerges as a new identity. Giving a fascinating insight into the club since the war this volume features over 230 illustrations.

0 7524 3107 2

If you are interested in purchasing other books published by The History Press, or in case you have difficulty finding any of our books in your local bookshop, you can also place orders directly through our website

www.thehistorypress.co.uk